Miracles and Modern Thought

About the Author
and Respondent

Norman L. Geisler

Norman L. Geisler is Professor of Systematic Theology at Dallas Theological Seminary. He is a graduate of Wheaton College (B.A. and M.A.), Detroit Bible College (Th.B.), and Loyola University (Ph.D.). Before coming to Dallas he was Professor of Philosophy of Religion and Chairman of the Department of Philosophy of Religion, Trinity Evangelical Divinity School, Deerfield. Among the books he has written are *Ethics: Alternatives and Issues; Philosophy of Religion; To Understand the Bible: Look for Jesus; Introduction to Philosophy: A Christian Perspective; Christian Apologetics; Inerrancy* (editor); and *Biblical Errancy: An Analysis of Its Philosophical Roots* (editor). Dr. Geisler is a member of the Evangelical Theological Society, American Philosophical Society, Evangelical Philosophical Society, and the American Scientific Affliliation and the American Academy of Religion.

R. C. Sproul

R. C. Sproul is President of Ligonier Valley Study Center near Stahlstown, Pennsylvania. He is a graduate of Westminster College (B.A.), Pittsburgh Theological Seminary (B.D.), and the Free University of Amsterdam (Drs.). He holds an honorary doctorate from Geneva College (Litt. D.). Dr. Sproul is the author of the following books: *The Symbol; The Psychology of Atheism; Discovering the Intimate Marriage; Knowing Scripture;* and *Objections Answered*. He is a member of the International Council on Biblical Inerrancy.

Miracles and Modern Thought

Norman L. Geisler

with a response by
R. C. Sproul

ZONDERVAN PUBLISHING HOUSE
OF THE ZONDERVAN CORPORATION
GRAND RAPIDS, MICHIGAN 49506

PROBE MINISTRIES
INTERNATIONAL
DALLAS, TEXAS 75251

Copyright   © 1982 by Probe Ministries International

**Library of
Congress
Cataloging in
Publication Data**

Geisler, Norman L.
    Miracles and modern thought.
    Bibliography: p.
    1. Miracles. I. Title.
BT97.2.G44   231.7'3   82-6999
                              AACR2

ISBN   0-310-44681-3

Scripture   Unless otherwise indicated, Scripture quotations are from
the New American Standard Bible, © 1960, 1962, 1963,
1968, 1971, 1972 by The Lockman Foundation.

First Printing   July 1982

**Place of
Printing**   *Printed in the United States of America*

Design   Cover design by Paul Lewis
Book design by Louise Bauer

What Is Probe?

Probe Ministries is a nonprofit corporation organized to provide perspective on the integration of the academic disciplines and historic Christianity. The members and associates of the Probe team are actively engaged in research as well as lecturing and interacting in thousands of university classrooms throughout the United States and Canada on topics and issues vital to the university student.

Christian Free University books should be ordered from Zondervan Publishing House (in the United Kingdom from the Paternoster Press), but further information about Probe's materials and ministries may be obtained by writing to Probe Ministries International, 12011 Coit Road, Suite 107, Dallas, Texas 75251.

Contents

Book Abstract

Today the naturalistic world view dominates both scientific and philosophical academic circles. This world view considers the possibility of miracles to be nonexistent or at least improbable. The author considers arguments from both the scientific and philosophical sides of naturalism, from the seventeenth century to the present, and demonstrates that naturalistic presuppositions rest on a commitment of faith.

Turning to the biblical world view, the author examines not only the possibility of miracles but also their purposefulness. He scrutinizes scientific and philosophical evidence for the veracity of the miracles reported in the New Testament. Finally, he gives detailed consideration to the context necessary to classify an event as a miracle.

chapter one

Are Miracles Possible?

Major philosophical objections to miracles from the seventeenth century to the present are reviewed. The thought of Benedict Spinoza, one of the first modern philosophers to object to the possibility of miracles, is analyzed.

Moses stretched out his hand over the waters and the Red Sea divided! Joshua spoke to the sun and it stopped in the middle of the sky for a whole day. Elisha made an iron axe float on the water! Jesus gave sight to the blind, caused the lame to walk, and raised his friend Lazarus from the dead. He also walked on water, turned water into wine, and multiplied a few loaves and some fish into food for five thousand! This is the world of the Bible. It is a world of miraculous and incredible events—a world almost totally foreign to the modern mind.

The modern world, by contrast, is a natural one. It is a world in which solid metal objects heavier than water always sink, as do people who step into water. 11

The modern world is one where water flows to its own level but does not form vertical walls. It is a world where dead remain in the grave and where winemakers cannot fill their wine barrels from the water faucet; they must wait for slow natural processes to produce wine from grapes. Indeed, the biblical world and the modern world are worlds apart. The one seems mythical and the other real. The one seems superstitious and the other scientific.

Whether or not people believe in miracles makes a big difference in their lives. Those with a background in traditional Judaism or Christianity accept a world and life view in which belief in the supernatural is an essential part. This includes millions of people who accept the possibility of miracles as part of their lives today. They pray for healing and even speak of supernatural "born again" experiences; for example, Chuck Colson who was involved in the Watergate scandal. For those who believe in the supernatural there is also a belief in future miracles. They speak, with Hal Lindsey, of "the late great planet earth" as coming to a supernatural climax with the literal return of Jesus Christ to set up an earthly utopia.

On the other hand, those who reject miracles often share Sigmund Freud's view that the miraculous is escapism or an illusion. They see it as a childhood neurosis that men vainly desire to protect themselves from the horrible realities of life. A famous atheist, Ludwig Feuerbach, firmly believed that such a belief in the supernatural sapped needed human energy from this world. His aim, therefore, was "to change the friends of God into friends of man, believers into thinkers, worshippers into workers, candidates for the other world into students of this world, Christians, who on their own confession are half animal and half angel, into men—whole men."[1]

Miracles and the Thinking Person

So it does make a significant difference in one's life as to whether or not miracles are credible. There is no question that people believed in the supernatural in ancient and medieval times and on through the Reformation. But, following the Renaissance and the

Enlightenment, it became increasingly difficult for the thinking person to maintain this belief.

Before we analyze whether miracles are credible, that is, before we find out whether miracles are possible, we must be clear as to what we mean by the term *miracle*. As Thomas Huxley has pointed out, "The first step in this, as in all other discussions, is to come to a clear understanding as to the meaning of the term employed. Argumentation about whether miracles are possible and, if possible, credible, is mere beating the air until the arguers have agreed what they mean by the word 'miracle.' "[2]

In brief, a miracle is a divine intervention into, or an interruption of, the regular course of the world that produces a purposeful but unusual event that would not (or could not) have occurred otherwise. The natural world is the world of regular, observable, and predictable events. Hence, a miracle by definition cannot be predicted by natural means.

In order to expand on our definition of the term *miracle*, we also need some initial understanding of what is meant by natural law. For a beginning description, natural law is understood as the usual, orderly, and general way that the world operates. It follows, then, that a miracle is an unusual, irregular, specific way in which God acts within the world. As Sir George Stokes, the famous physicist who discovered the laws that now bear his name, has said, "It may be that the event which we call a miracle was brought about not by the suspension of the laws in ordinary operation, but by the superaddition of something not ordinarily in operation."[3] In other words, if a miracle occurs, it would not be a violation or contradiction of the ordinary laws of cause and effect, but a *new effect* produced by the introduction of a supernatural cause.

Keeping that definition of miracles in mind, this book will examine the most important philosophers in the miracles debate. We do this in order to get a closer look at the reasons why so many reject the credibility of miracles and to understand why it has become so difficult for the thinking person to seriously maintain belief in the supernatural. One of the reasons for this difficulty emanates from the philosophy of the famous seventeenth-century Jewish philosopher, Benedict Spinoza (1632-1677). Arguing from a strong rationalistic perspective, Spinoza did not hesitate to pronounce the belief in miracles absurd.

Spinoza was one of the early rationalists, a gifted and brilliant philosopher who developed a complete form of pantheism. A lens-grinder by trade, Spinoza was so original and unorthodox in his thinking that his views caused him to be expelled from the Jewish synagogue at age twenty-four.

His significance in the history of philosophy and particularly on the issue of miracles lies in his view of the nature of God. Spinoza believed that there could be only one infinite substance, and that therefore the universe was uncreated. In other words, God is identical with the universe. He could not have created it, for it is of His essence. For Spinoza, God is not transcendent, He is not beyond or "other" than creation. This means, then, in Spinoza's view, that God's creativity is no more than nature's activity. If Spinoza's presupposition is true, miracles are impossible. For if God (the supernatural) is identical to nature, then it follows that there is no supernatural intervention *into* nature from anything beyond it. Knowing this general framework, we will now examine Spinoza's arguments against miracles.

I. The Impossibility of Miracles

Spinoza declared about nature that "nothing then, comes to pass in nature in contravention to her universal laws, nay, nothing does not agree with them and follow from them, for . . . she keeps a fixed and immutable order." In fact "a miracle, whether in contravention to, or beyond, nature, is a mere absurdity." Spinoza was nothing short of dogmatic about the impossibility of miracles. He unashamedly proclaimed, "We may, then, be absolutely certain that every event which is truly described in Scripture necessarily happened, like everything else, according to natural laws."[4]

A. *The Character of Spinoza's Argument*

When one reduces Spinoza's argument against miracles to its basic premise it seems to go something like this:

1. Miracles are violations of natural laws.
2. Natural laws are immutable.
3. It is impossible for immutable laws to be violated.
4. Therefore, miracles are impossible.

The second premise is the key to Spinoza's argument. Nature "keeps a fixed and *immutable* order."[5] Everything "*necessarily* happened . . . according to natural laws."[6] He believed that "nothing comes to pass in nature in contravention to her [nature's] *universal* laws. . . ."[7] (Emphases in these statements are mine.) If this were true, then Spinoza would be right; to believe otherwise "is a mere absurdity."[8]

In order to appreciate what Spinoza meant, one must be aware that he was a rationalist who tried to construct his philosophy on the model of Euclid's geometry.[9] That is, he believed that one should accept as true only what is self-evident or what is reducible to the self-evident. In other words, like René Descartes, he argued in a geometric way from axioms to conclusions contained in these axioms. Spinoza lived in an age increasingly impressed with the orderliness of a physical universe. Because of this it was apparently axiomatic to Spinoza that natural laws are immutable.

B. *The Consequence of Spinoza's Argument*

Spinoza's rationalism had far-reaching consequences for anyone who believes in either miraculous events or supernatural revelations. In point of fact, Spinoza became one of the first thinkers to engage in a systematic higher criticism of the Bible. His *Tractatus*, widely circulated in the late seventeenth century, was chiefly a critical commentary of the Bible. Through Spinoza's argument in the *Tractatus* and his other writings we see that he came to some radical conclusions. If these conclusions are true, then the orthodox Christian view, that the Scriptures are totally inspired by God, is false. So we must first view his conclusions in order to evaluate his whole argument fairly.

First of all, Spinoza's naturalistic rationalism led him to conclude that since "there are many passages in the Pentateuch which Moses could not have written, it follows that the belief that Moses was the author of the Pentateuch is ungrounded and even irrational."[10] Who wrote the first five books of the Old Testament? The same person, said Spinoza, who wrote the rest of the Old Testament: Ezra the scribe.[11]

Second, Spinoza eliminated the resurrection accounts from the Gospels. Concerning Christianity he said that "the Apostles who came after Christ, preached it to all men as a universal religion *solely* in virtue of Christ's Passion" (emphasis mine).[12] In other words, Spinoza reduced Christianity to a mystical, nonpropositional religion, a religion without foundations. Orthodox Christianity has held, since the apostle Paul, that apart from the truth of the resurrection of Christ, Christianity is a religion without hope.

Third, for Spinoza, the Scripture merely "*contains* the word of God . . ." (emphasis mine).[13] Here his influence continues today, since the debate concerning the character of the Bible still centers around this crucial issue. In Spinoza's view, it is false to say, as orthodox Christians have, that the Bible *is* the word. For him the parts of the Bible that contain the word of God are known to be such because the morality conforms to a natural law known by human reason.[14]

Fourth, Spinoza makes a categorical denial of all miracles in the Bible. Spinoza commends "anyone who seeks for the true causes of miracles and strives to understand natural phenomena as an intelligent being. . . ."[15] Not only did he conclude that "every event . . . in Scripture necessarily happened, like everything else, according to natural laws,"[16] but that Scripture itself "makes the general assertion in several passages that nature's course is *fixed and unchangeable*" (emphasis mine).[17]

Finally, he said that the prophets did not speak from supernatural "revelation" and "the modes of expression and discourse adopted by the Apostles in the Epistles, show very clearly that the latter were not written by revelation and Divine command, but *merely by the natural powers* and judgment of the authors"[18] (emphasis mine).

Not everyone would agree with Spinoza's wholesale rationalistic rejection of miracles. However, both his antisupernaturalism and general criticism of the Bible are still widely held today by secular scholars and liberal Christian scholars as well.

II. THE UNACCEPTABILITY OF SPINOZA'S CRITIQUE

Spinoza's attack on miracles rests squarely on three foundations: his "Euclidian" (geometric, or deductive) rationalism, his "Newtonian" view of natural laws, and his view of the nature of God. All three of these are subject to serious criticism and none can be rationally *proved*. In any event, we will see that each falls far short as a definitive argument against miracles.

A. *Spinoza's Deductive Deck Is Stacked*

As to Spinoza's "Euclidian" (deductive) rationalism, it suffers from an acute case of *petitio principii* (begging the question), for anything validly deducible from premises must have already been present in those premises to begin with. But if the antisupernatural is already presupposed in Spinoza's rationalistic premises, then it is no surprise to discover him attacking the miracles of the Bible. What is really at stake is the truth of the rationalistic premises for which Spinoza has no rational proof, at least none that is sound, to say nothing of convincing, even to most other naturalists. In other words, once one defines natural law as "fixed," "immutable," and "unchangeable," then it is certainly irrational to say a miracle occurred. How can anything break the unbreakable?

B. *Spinoza's Closed Universe Untenable*

Further, Spinoza's concept of natural law, based on Newtonian physics, is scientifically untenable. For Spinoza, nature was a "closed system" and, hence, law describes the way things *must* behave. For most contemporary scientists, the universe is an "open system" in which natural laws are merely statistical averages or probabilities of the ways things *do* behave. If so, then there is always, from the scientific perspective, the *possibility* that there may be exceptions to these "normal" patterns. In this way a miraculous event would only be viewed as an anomaly, not a violation of immutable law. Hence, in contemporary scientific discussion, we cannot dismiss miracles as impossible *by definition*, as Spinoza does.

C. *Spinoza's God and Modern Science*

Of course, miracles as acts of God in the natural world cannot actually occur unless the theistic God exists, rather than the pantheistic god of Spinoza. Hence, scientists will want evidence that God exists before they are likely to believe in miracles. Is there any scientific evidence for this belief? And what of Spinoza's view of the nature of God?

One of the most incredible situations in modern science was recently described by a highly respected astrophysicist, Robert Jastrow. He tells of the reluctance of brilliant scientists to conclude that the universe came into existence with a "Big Bang" some alleged billions of years ago. Jastrow offers several lines of scientific evidence that support a beginning of the universe: the fact that the universe is running down (and thus cannot be eternal), the fact that the universe is expanding from its original explosion (even the radiation "echo" of the original explosion has allegedly been discovered), and Einstein's theory of relativity. The discovery of the radiation "echo," writes Jastrow, "has convinced almost the last doubting Thomas. . . ."[19] Concerning this, he continues, "Theologians generally are delighted with the

proof that the universe had a beginning, but astronomers are curiously upset."[20]

A most notable example of how brilliant scientists
become upset at these findings is the case of Albert
Einstein. Einstein developed the general theory of relativity but failed to observe that an expanding universe followed as a conclusion from this theory. The
Russian mathematician Alexander Friedmann pointed
out that Einstein's failure to conclude that the universe had a beginning came about because he "had
made a *schoolboy error* in algebra . . ." (emphasis
mine). In effect,[21] he had divided by zero! What did
the scientific genius Einstein do when Friedmann
pointed out his error? He defended his thesis by a
"proof" that made another mistake!

Eventually Einstein recognized his error and wrote,
"My objection rested on an error in calculation. I
consider Mr. Friedmann's results to be correct and
illuminating."[22] However, "this circumstance [of an
expanding universe] irritated me." In another place
he said, "To admit such possibilities seems senseless."[23]

Just why would such a brilliant mathematical mind
consider "senseless" the view that the universe had a
beginning, and how was he "irritated" into making a
simple mathematical error? Part of the answer, says
Jastrow, lies in Einstein's philosophical conception of
God and the universe. In 1921 a rabbi sent Einstein a
telegram asking, "Do you believe in God?" to which
Einstein answered, "*I believe in Spinoza's God*, who
reveals himself in the orderly harmony of what
exists" (emphasis mine).[24] This explains why Einstein could not believe in a supernatural beginning of
the universe. As we have seen, Spinoza was a
rationalist for whom God's essence is equated with
the universe and for whom the universe is eternal and
operates only according to the uniformity of natural
law.

Today we have scientific evidence that the universe
is of finite age, i.e., had a beginning. Therefore, for
rational minds creation would seem to be the only

alternative. Why? As William James pointed out, "From nothing to being there is no logical bridge."[25] And it makes no sense to say, with C. F. Weizsäcker, that all things have come from "nothingness pregnant with being,"[26] since "nothing" means nonbeing. In view of the increasing evidence, the British physicist Edmund Whittaker concluded, "It is simpler to postulate creation *ex nihilo*—divine will constituting Nature from nothingness."[*27]

Unscientific Reactions

Despite this scientific evidence for a creation (and Creator!), many scientists strongly resist this conclusion. In 1931 Eddington wrote, "The expanding universe is preposterous . . . incredible. . . . *It leaves me cold.*"[28] More recently Phillip Morrison of M.I.T. said, "I find it hard to accept the Big Bang theory; *I would like to reject it.*"[29] Even Allan Sandage of Palomar Observatory said, "It is such a strange conclusion. . . . It cannot really be true."[30]

But despite these unscientific reactions, the scientist is being upset by his own scientific discoveries. Jastrow concludes: "For the scientist who has lived by faith in the power of reason, the story ends like a bad dream. He has scaled the mountain of ignorance; he is about to conquer the highest peak; as he pulls himself over the final rock, he is greeted by a band of theologians who have been sitting there for centuries."[31]

---

*Some have suggested a winding and rewinding process going on forever, but there are several problems with this. First, Jastrow notes that the creation (from nothing) of fresh hydrogen atoms are necessary for the "rewinding" process. But contrary to Jastrow's own agnosticism about how this occurred, this would necessitate postulating a God to create them (nothing cannot produce something). Secondly, it is impossible to have an actual infinite series of events (of "winding" and "unwinding") going backwards, since no matter how many there were, one more could always be added. Potential or abstract (mathematical) infinite series are possible, but not actual, concrete ones. For instance, one cannot have a chain with an actually infinite number of links. Finally, even if the universe were "bouncing back" in seemingly endless rebounds, the second law of thermodynamics would indicate that it would not "rebound" as far each time. Hence, the universe will run down anyway—it will just take longer.

Modern philosophy and science since even before the Enlightenment cast serious doubt on the ancient belief in miracles. Spinoza had been a precursor of the attack. But when his arguments are examined carefully, they are found wanting, both in the light of their philosophical presuppositions and in view of findings in contemporary science.

Spinoza's argument fails because, first, it begs the question by *defining* miracles as impossible to begin with, namely as a violation of assumed unbreakable natural laws. What Spinoza needed to do, but did not, was to provide some sound argument *for his rationalistic presuppositions*. In short, his reasoning is geometric, but his rationalistic "axioms" are wrong. Second, Spinoza's concept of natural law as a closed system is scientifically untenable. Today's scientists accept the "open" system as more feasible because it better provides for the explanation of exceptions to natural law. Therefore, miracles cannot be pronounced impossible by definition.

Finally, the scientific evidence is mounting for a supernatural creation of the space-time universe. If this is so, then the beginning of the universe would be a prime example of a kind of miracle! Further, concluding that the universe had a beginning provides a devastating blow to Spinoza's concept of God, and calls into question the naturalistic view that no God exists and that miracles are impossible. Rather than arguing against miracles, science may be coming (however reluctantly) to the defense of the supernatural.

Are Miracles
Possible?

**Summarizing
the Critique
of Spinoza**

chapter two

Are Miracles Incredible?

The empirical epistemology of David Hume is examined and two major arguments against miracles from his famous Inquiry *are presented. A critique of these examines the consistency of Hume's argument with his own epistemology.*

While few current thinkers accept the rationalistic basis from which Spinoza launched his attack on miracles, they have by no means expressed a willingness to return to a pre-Enlightenment belief in the supernatural. Most modern thinkers who reject miracles would trace their reasons to those of the famous Scottish skeptic, David Hume. The reason for this is simple: he has provided what many believe to be the most formidable of all challenges to a supernaturalist perspective.

I. THE BASIS FOR HUME'S CRITIQUE OF MIRACLES

David Hume (1711–1776) was a Scottish philosopher and historian, born and reared in Edinburgh. He graduated from Edinburgh University with a degree in law but soon after decided not to practice. Instead,   23 during the height of the European Enlightenment, Hume took up a rigorous study of philosophy. This study led to his definitive system of naturalism and a disdain for any system that provided for the existence of God or the miraculous. His significance for any study of miracles lay in his epistemological method and his view of natural law; like Spinoza, he was Newtonian.

However, unlike Spinoza, Hume attacked miracles not from a rationalistic perspective but from an empirical one. In many ways the two men were opposites. Spinoza was dogmatic and Hume was skeptical. Spinoza was rationalistic and a priori; Hume was experiential and a posteriori.* These differences notwithstanding, the result is the same—it is unreasonable to believe that miracles occur. There is, however, an important difference to note. For Spinoza, miracles are actually impossible; for Hume, they are merely incredible.

A. Hume's Empirical Skepticism

Hume believed that "all the objects of human reason or inquiry may naturally be divided into two kinds, to wit, '*Relations of Ideas*,' and '*Matters of Fact*.'"[32] The first kind includes mathematical statements and definitions; the second class includes everything known empirically, that is, through one or more of the five senses. So emphatic was Hume about this distinction that he concluded his famous *Inquiry* with these words:

> When we run over libraries, persuaded of these principles, what havoc must we make? If we take in our hand any volume—of divinity or school metaphysics, for instance—let us ask, *Does it contain any abstract reasoning concerning quantity or number?* No. *Does it contain any experimental reasoning concerning matter of fact and existence?* No. Commit it then to the flames, for it can contain nothing but sophistry and illusion.[33]

---

*Things known a priori are known *prior to* or independent of experience. Things known a posteriori are know *from* (after) experience.

For Hume "all reasonings concerning matter of fact seem to be founded on the relation of *cause* and *effect*. By means of that relation alone we can go beyond the evidence of our memory and senses."[34] In view of this, the mind can never find the cause for a given event. Only "after the constant conjunction of two objects, heat and flame, for instance . . . we are determined by *custom alone* to expect the one from the appearance of the other" (emphasis mine).[35] That is, we make use of causality, but we have no empirical grounds for doing so. In short, one cannot know causal *connections* between things; one can only believe in them based on customary *conjunctions*. "All inferences from experience, therefore, are effects of custom, not of reasoning. . . ."[36]

According to Hume, we cannot even be sure the sun will rise tomorrow. We can (and do) *believe* it will, because it has customarily risen in the past. Of course, some things happen so often in conjunction that it is foolish not to believe they will be so conjoined in the future. Hume would even call this uniform experience a "proof," by which he means "such arguments from experience as leave no room for doubt or opposition."[37] Nonetheless, "all events seem entirely loose and separate. One event follows another; but we never can observe any tie between them. They seem *conjoined*, but never *connected*."[38] Merely conjoining does not prove causal connection any more than there is a causal connection between the rooster crowing and the sun rising! One must extrapolate based on oft-repeated occurrences.

II. HUME'S CLAIM: THE INCREDIBILITY OF MIRACLES

Building on this empirical epistemology, Hume launched his attack on miracles in Part X of his famous *Inquiry*.*

---

*Hume actually has two arguments against miracles here. The first argument is an argument *in principle,* which assumes the credibility of witnesses. The second is an argument *in practice,* which challenges in fact whether any miracles have ever had credible witnesses. (The latter will be considered in chapter 11.)

In introducing his argument, Hume comments, "I flatter myself that I have discovered an argument . . . which, if just, will, with the wise and learned, be an everlasting check to all kinds of superstitious delusion, and consequently will be useful as long as the world endures."[39] What is this "final" argument against miracles? In Hume's own words the reasoning goes like this:

1. "A wise man . . . proportions his belief to the evidence."[40]

2. "If such conclusions are founded on an infallible experience, he expects the event with the last degree of assurance and regards his past experience as a full *proof* of the future existence of that event."[41]

3. "As the evidence derived from witnesses and human testimony is founded on past experience, so it varies with the experience and is regarded either as a *proof* or a *probability*, according as the conjunction between any particular kind of report and any kind of object has been found to be constant or variable."[42]

4. "There are a number of circumstances to be taken into consideration in all judgments of this kind; and the ultimate standard by which we determine all disputes that may arise concerning them is always derived from experience and observation."[43]

5. "Where this experience is not entirely uniform on any side, it is attended with an unavoidable contrariety in our judgments and with the same opposition and mutual destruction of argument as in every other kind of evidence."[44]

6. "We entertain a suspicion concerning any matter of fact when the witnesses contradict each other, when they are but few or of a doubtful character, when they have an interest in what they affirm, when they deliver their testimony with hesitation or . . . with too violent asseverations."[45]

7. "But when the fact attested is such a one as has seldom fallen under our observation, here is a contest of two opposite experiences; of which the one destroys the other as far as its force goes, and the superior can only operate on the mind by the force which remains."[46]

8. "A miracle is a violation of the laws of nature; and . . . firm and unalterable experience has established these laws. . . ."[47]

9. Therefore, "the proof against a miracle, from the very nature of the fact, is as entire as any argument from experience can possibly be imagined."[48]

10. Since "a uniform experience amounts to a proof, there is here a direct and full *proof*, from the nature of the fact, against the existence of any miracle."[49]

One can abbreviate Hume's argument considerably:

Abbreviating Hume's Argument

1. "A miracle is a violation of the laws of nature."

2. "Firm and unalterable experience has established these laws [of nature]."

3. "A wise man proportions his belief to the evidence."

4. Therefore, "the proof against miracles . . . is as entire as any argument from experience can possibly be imagined."

In summary, Hume wrote, "There must, therefore, be a uniform experience against every miraculous event. Otherwise the event would not merit that appellation." So "nothing is esteemed a miracle if it ever happened in the common course of nature."[50]

B. *Two Ways to Understand Hume's Argument*

There are two basic ways to understand Hume's argument against miracles. We will call these the "hard" and "soft" interpretations. According to the "hard" interpretation of the argument, Hume would be saying:

1. Miracles by definition are a violation of natural law.
2. Natural laws are unalterably uniform.
3. Therefore, miracles cannot occur.

Now, despite the fact that Hume's argument sometimes sounds like this, it is not necessarily what he has in mind. If this is his argument, then it clearly begs the question by simply defining miracles as impossible. For if miracles are a "violation" of what cannot be "altered," then miracles are ipso facto* impossible. There is a way, however, that a supernaturalist could avoid this dilemma. He could refuse to define miracles as a "violation" of fixed law and simply call it an "exception" to a general rule. That is, he could define natural law as the regular (normal) pattern of events but not the universal or unalterable pattern. But this would be an easy way out of the problem for the supernaturalist. Hume's real argument is much more difficult to answer. It is not an argument for the impossibility of miracles but for the *incredibility* of miracles. It can be stated this way:

1. A miracle is by definition a rare occurrence.
2. Natural law is by definition a description of a regular occurrence.
3. The evidence for the regular is always greater than that for the rare.
4. A wise man always bases his belief on the greater evidence.
5. Therefore, a wise man should never believe in miracles.

**Evaluating
Hume's "Soft"
Argument**

Notice that on this "soft" form of the argument miracles are not ruled out entirely; they are simply held to be always incredible by the very nature of the evidence. The wise man does not claim that miracles cannot occur; he simply never *believes* they happen, because he never has enough evidence for that belief.†

---

*Ipso facto means "by the very nature of the case."

†The indications that Hume is stressing credibility (or believability) is found in his use of the terms "belief," "is esteemed,"

However, even in this "soft" interpretation of the argument, miracles are still eliminated, since by the *very nature of the case* no thoughtful person should ever hold that a miracle has indeed occurred. If this is so, Hume has seemingly avoided begging the question and yet has successfully eliminated the possibility of reasonable belief in miracles. Variations of these arguments are still held to be valid by some widely respected contemporary philosophers. (See chapter 5 where Antony Flew's reformulation of Hume's argument is discussed.)

III. ANSWERING HUME'S ARGUMENTS AGAINST MIRACLES

Since the "hard" form of Hume's argument clearly begs the question and is easily answered by redefining the terms, we will concentrate primarily on the "soft" form for the purpose of this evaluation. In order to proceed, a word of evaluation about Hume's claim for "uniform experience" is necessary.

A. *Is All Experience Uniform?*

Hume speaks of "uniform" experience against miracles, but this either begs the question or else is special pleading. It begs the question if Hume presumes to know the experience is uniform *in advance* of looking at the evidence. For how can one know that all *possible* experience will confirm his naturalism, unless he has access to all possible experiences, including those in the future? If, on the other hand, Hume simply means by "uniform" experience that select experiences of *some* persons (who have not encountered a miracle), then this is special pleading. For there are others who claim to have experienced miracles.

In the final analysis, then, the debate over miracles cannot be settled by supposed "uniform" experience. For this either begs the question in advance or else opens the door for a factual analysis of whether in-

**No "Uniform"
Settlement**

"testimony," and "probability" and also in his definition of natural law, namely, the believed conjunction based on customary (repeated) experience.

deed there is sufficient evidence to believe that a miracle has occurred. As C. S. Lewis observed,

> Now of course we must agree with Hume that if there is absolutely "uniform experience" against miracles, if in other words they have never happened, why then they never have. Unfortunately we know the experience against them to be uniform only if we know that all the reports of them are false. And we can know all the reports to be false only if we know already that miracles have never occurred. In fact, we are arguing in a circle.[51] The only alternative to this circular arguing is *to be open to the possibility that miracles have occurred*.

B. *Is the Evidence Always Stronger Against Miracles?*

Hume is certainly correct in affirming "a wise man . . . proportions his belief to the evidence."[52] But is he right in assuming "there is here a direct and full proof . . . against the existence of any miracle"?*[53]

At the basis of Hume's concept of what amounts to superior "evidence" is his concept of "custom" and constant conjunction. Since causal connections cannot be known, one must simply *believe* in the connection based on constant (repeated) conjunction. When the events occur together over and over again, this customary conjunction gives greater and greater credibility to our belief that there is a causal connection. So, in the final analysis, "greater evidence" for Hume means *events that are more often repeated*. This is why a rare event (like a miracle) can *never* have as much evidence in its favor as can a regular event (such as a falling object) for, by virtue of the fact that it is rare by definition, it must thereby be evidentially weaker.

There are several serious problems with this understanding of "evidence." First, it too begs the question. For if in principle one knows *in advance* (before ever weighing the evidence) that the evidence against miracles will always be greater, then of course no reasonable person should believe in miracles. In fact,

---

*Actually, Hume was inconsistent with his own view, since he admitted there may be sufficient evidence to prove a unique event such as an eclipse.

Hume does not really "weigh" evidence for miracles; he really *adds* evidence against them. Since death occurs over and over and over again and resurrection occurs only on rare occasions, we simply "add" up all the deaths against the very few alleged resurrections and reject the latter. In Hume's own words, "It is no miracle that a man, seemingly in good health, should die on a sudden, because such a kind of death . . . has yet been frequently observed to happen. But it is a miracle that a dead man should come to life; because that has never been observed in any age or country." Hence, "it is more probable that all men must die. . . ."[54]

✔

Hume's Fallacy

There is another problem with Hume's concept of adding up events to determine truth. First of all, even if a few resurrections *actually occurred*, according to Hume's principles one should not believe them, since the number of deaths would always outweigh them. However, truth is not determined by majority vote. Hume here commits a kind of *consensus gentium.**

Second, this argument really equates "evidence" and "probability." It says in effect that one should always believe what is most probable, that is, that which has the highest "odds." On these grounds one should not believe the dice he rolled shows three sixes if he gets them on the first roll, since the odds against it are 216 to 1. Or, one should not believe he was dealt a perfect bridge hand (which has happened) since the odds against it are 1,635,013,559,600 to 1! What Hume overlooks is that the wise people base their beliefs on *facts*, not on odds. Sometimes the "odds" against an event are high (based on past observation), but the evidence for the event is very good (based on contemporary observation or testimony).

Finally, Hume's concept of "adding" evidence proves too much. It proves that one should not believe *any* unusual or unique event from the past, to say nothing of miracles. Richard Whately satirized

---

*An informal fallacy: that which is believed by most people carries the weight of truth.

Hume's thesis in his famous pamphlet, *Historical Doubts Concerning the Existence of Napoleon Bonaparte*. Since Napoleon's exploits were so fantastic, so extraordinary, so unprecedented, no intelligent person should believe that these events ever happened. After recounting Napoleon's amazing and unparalleled military feats, Whately wrote, "Does anyone believe all this and yet refuse to believe a miracle? Or rather, what is this but a miracle? Is not this a violation of the laws of nature?" If the skeptic does not deny the existence of Napoleon, he "must at least acknowledge that they do not apply to that question the same plan of reasoning which they have made use of in others. . . ."[55]

C. *Can One Eliminate Belief in Present Events Based on Evidence for Past Events?*

**Believing
in Advance**

It would seem that Hume wants the wise man always to *believe* in advance that miracles will never occur. Even before one examines the evidence, he should come "pre-armed" with the "uniform" and "unalterable" testimony of the past, so that even if the event seems highly miraculous, it should not be presumed to be a miracle. For "in such conclusions as are founded on an infallible experience, he expects the event with the last [i.e., highest] degree of assurance and regards his past experience as a full *proof* of the future existence of that event."[56]

But here again Hume's uniformitarian belief is revealed. For only if one approaches the future with a kind of invincible bias, that one should believe in accordance with what has been perceived in the past, can he discount all claims for the miraculous.

There are two important objections to this reasoning. First, Hume is inconsistent with his own epistemology. Hume himself recognized the fallacy of this kind of reasoning when he argued that, based on past conformity, nothing can be known as true concerning the future. We cannot even know for sure that the sun will rise tomorrow morning.[57] Hence, for Hume to deny future miracles (e.g., the future resurrection) based on past experience is inconsistent with his own principles and a violation of his own system.

Second, if it were true that no present exception can overthrow "laws" based on our uniform experience in the past, then there could be no true progress in our scientific understanding of the world. For established or repeatable exceptions to past patterns are precisely what force a change in scientific belief. When an observed exception to a past "law" is established, that "law" (L^1) is revised and a new "law" (L^2) replaces it. This is precisely what happened when certain outer-spatial "exceptions" to Newton's law of gravitation were found and Einstein's relativity was considered broader and more adequate. Without these established exceptions, no progress would have been made. In short, Hume's objections to miracles are unscientific! Exceptions to "laws" have a heuristic (discovery) value; they are goals to progress in our understanding of the universe.

SUMMARY AND CONCLUSION

Hume offered a forceful argument against miracles. But, strong as it may seem, the evaluation indicates he was overly optimistic to believe this argument could be "an everlasting check" and "useful as long as the world endures" to refute any credible claim for the miraculous. In point of fact, for several reasons Hume's argument is not successful. First, in the "hard" form he begs the question by assuming miracles are *by definition* impossible. Second, in the "soft" form of the argument Hume special pleads, begs the question, proves too much (such as, that even Napoleon didn't exist!), is inconsistent with his own epistemology, and makes scientific progress impossible. In brief, to eliminate miracles before looking at them seems prejudicial, and not to do this is to leave the door open to their possibility. A wise person does not *legislate* in advance that miracles *cannot* be believed to have happened; rather he *looks* at the evidence to see if they *did* occur. So, for the rational mind, Hume's efforts to eliminate miracles must be considered unsuccessful.

This does not mean, however, that there are no

chapter three

Are Miracles Repeatable?

The arguments of two modern philosophers, Chryssides and Flew, against the repeatability of miracles are reviewed and analyzed in light of their presuppositions. The supernaturalist's position on the repeatability of miracles is clarified.

The problems with Hume's objections to miracles notwithstanding, the "enlightened" or "scientific" mind has found it necessary to reject the supernatural. One outstanding contemporary example is the British philosopher Antony Flew.

As the arguments against miracles proceed, it becomes more obvious that the matter is not simply a factual one; it is a matter of life. While ancient and medieval man lived in a world of miracles, modern man has, by the scientific method, been content to extend his own control over the world in lieu of any alleged supernatural intervention. These "scientific" objections are stated well by Flew.

35

I. Flew's Argument for Unrepeatability

Born in London in 1923, Flew has been a lecturer in philosophy at three major British universities, including Oxford and Aberdeen. Currently he is a professor of philosophy at the University of Keele. As a contemporary philosopher of the analytical school, Flew is well known in the philosophical world for his works in philosophical theology. He has authored and edited numerous books and articles in scholarly journals and has been especially recognized for his arguments against miracles (particularly his article on "Miracles" in the *Encyclopedia of Philosophy*). He argues against miracles on the grounds that they are unrepeatable.

A. *The Statement of Flew's Argument*

As Flew sees it, Hume's argument really amounts to something like this:

1. Every miracle is a violation of a law of nature.
2. The evidence against any violation of nature is the strongest possible evidence.
3. Therefore, the evidence against miracles is the strongest possible evidence.

Flew says that "Hume was primarily concerned, not with the question of fact, but with that of evidence. The problem was how the occurrence of a miracle could be proved, rather than whether any such events had ever occurred." However, adds Flew, "our sole ground for characterizing the reported occurrence as miraculous is at the same time a sufficient reason for calling it physically impossible." Why, we may ask, is this so? Because "the critical historian, confronted with some story of a miracle, will usually dismiss it out of hand. . . ." On what grounds? Flew answers, "To justify his procedure he will have to appeal to precisely the principle which Hume advanced: the 'absolute impossibility or miraculous nature' of the events attested must, 'in the eyes of all reasonable people . . . alone be regarded as a sufficient refutation.'" In short, even though miracles are not *logically impossible, they are sci-*

entifically impossible. "For it is only and precisely by presuming that the laws that hold today held in the past . . . that we can rationally interpret the *detritus* [fragments] of the past as evidence and from it construct our account of what actually happened."[58]

As to the charge that this uniformitarian approach to history is "irrationally dogmatic," Flew answers with what is really the heart of his amplification of Hume's argument. First, "as Hume was insisting from first to last, the possibility of miracles is a matter of evidence and not of dogmatism." Further, "the proposition reporting the (alleged) occurrence of the miracle will be singular, particular, and in the past tense. . . ." Propositions of this sort "cannot any longer be tested directly. It is this that gives propositions of the first sort [i.e., of the general and repeatable] the vastly greater logical strength. . . ."[59] In view of this, Flew's argument can now be stated as follows:

1. Miracles are by nature particular and unrepeatable.
2. Natural events are by nature general and repeatable.
3. Now, in practice, the evidence for the general and repeatable is always greater than that for the particular and unrepeatable.
4. Therefore, in practice, the evidence will always be greater against miracles than for them.

With this statement it becomes clear that for Flew *generality* and *repeatability* (in the present) are what give natural events greater evidential value than miracles. And since, of course, it will always be this way in the future, the evidence against miracles will always be greater than the evidence for them.

B. *An Evaluation of Flew's Argument*

There are several things that should be observed about Flew's argument. First, it begs the question to assume that miracles must be viewed as *past* events. Flew seems to assume *without proof* that miracles are not occurring in the present. By consigning them to the unrepeatable past, Flew would thereby automatically minimize their evidential value, since they are not available for present scrutiny. This, however, is not valid, since there is stronger evidence for some unrepeatable things in the past (e.g., World War II) than for some repeatable things in the present (e.g., whether I can hit a hole-in-one). Second, Flew assumes that miracles are in no sense *general* or *repeatable*. Actually, the Bible claims that Jesus performed many miracles of healing (and even resurrections) over and over again. Further, miracles do not have to be repeated in order to be repeatable. If there is a God, then presumably He could repeat miracles as He wills. Third, no event is really general. Each event is unique, even though it may be similar to others. If this is so, then, strictly speaking, the evidence would be no greater for one event than for another.

Fourth, most modern naturalists, such as Flew, accept some irrepeatable singularities of their own. Many contemporary astronomers believe in the singular origin of the universe by a "Big Bang." And nearly all scientists believe that the origin of life on this planet is a singular event that has never been repeated here. But if Flew's argument against miracles is correct, then it is also wrong for scientists to believe in these singularities that many of them consider to be natural events. Thus Flew's argument against supernaturalism would also eliminate some basic naturalistic belief(s).

Fifth, Flew's view is subject to his own criticism of Christians, namely, it is an *unfalsifiable* position. For no matter what state of affairs actually occurs (even a resurrection), Flew (contrary even to Hume's claims) would be obliged to believe it was *not* a miracle. Elsewhere, Flew argued that "it often seems to people who are not religious as if there was no conceivable event or series of events the occurrence of which would be admitted by sophisticated religious people to be a sufficient reason for conceding 'there wasn't a God after all. . . .' " In short, their belief is in actuality unfalsifiable. But in like manner we may ask Flew (rephrasing his own words), "What would have to occur or to have occurred to constitute for you a disproof of . . . your antisupernaturalism?"[60] The answer is: No event in the world would do so for Flew, because *in practice* he believes the evidence is always greater against miracles than for them.

It will not help for Flew to admit that his antisupernaturalism is falsifiable in *principle* but never in practice, on the grounds that in practice the evidence will always be greater for the repeatable. For surely he would then have to allow the theist to claim that, in principle, the existence of God is falsifiable but that, in practice, no event could disconfirm God's existence! The fact that Flew and other nontheists busy themselves to disprove God by arguing from the *fact* of evil in the world reveals their belief that falsification *in practice* is that with which they are really concerned.

The truth is that Flew cannot have it both ways. If naturalism is unfalsifiable in practice, then belief in God (or in miracles) can also be unfalsifiable in practice. On the other hand, if supernaturalism can never be established in practice, then neither can naturalism be so established. For it is always possible for the theist to claim of *every* alleged natural event that "God is the ultimate cause of it." The theist may insist that all "natural" events (i.e., naturally repeatable ones) are the way God *normally* operates and the "miraculous" events are the way He works on *special* occasions. Now, on Flew's own grounds, there is no way *in practice* to falsify this theistic belief. For, again, just as Flew claimed for naturalism that it is unfalsifiable in practice, so too the theist could claim the same. For no matter what events in the natural world are produced (repeatable or unrepeatable), the theist can still claim "God is the ultimate cause of it," and, on Flew's grounds, no naturalist can disprove this theistic claim.*

Sixth, one may object to Flew's assumption that the repeatable always evidentially outweighs the unrepeatable. If this were so, then as Richard Whately pointed out (see chapter 2), one could not believe in the historicity of *any* unusual events from the past (none of which are repeatable). In fact, if repeatability in practice is the true test of superior evidence, then one should not believe that observed births or deaths occurred, for a person's birth and death are both unrepeatable in practice. Likewise, even historical geology is unrepeatable in practice. Hence, if Flew were right, the science of geology should be eliminated too!

It will not avail for the naturalist to claim that births and deaths in *general* are repeatable (even though particular ones are not), for the supernaturalist can claim that miracles in general can be repeated, too. In fact, according to the Bible, many miracles have been repeated over and over. Nor will it avail to claim that one can always specify the conditions in advance for a natural event but never for a miracle. First of all, one cannot always specify in advance when a natural event will occur. We do not know in advance when Don Jones will lift his arm, but we know that when he does the naturalist will claim it is not a supernatural event. If the naturalist replies that when Jones will lift his arm can be specified *in principle* (but not in practice, namely, when Jones deems it desirable to do so), then the theist can also specify in principle and in advance when a miracle will occur. It will occur when God deems it desirable to perform one! Thus the de-

---

*It will not do for the naturalist to attempt a *reductio ad absurdum* and insist that if God causes *all* natural events, then He causes evil (e.g., tornadoes). For this argument begs the question in assuming that God has no good purpose for these natural events. (And then this premise could be known for certain to be true only if the atheist is omniscient.) Further, the theist denies that God is the cause of evil (for which He has a good purpose); the immediate cause of evil is some free agent(s) God permits to operate for an ultimate good known to Himself. (For further discussion of this point, see my *Roots of Evil* [Grand Rapids: Zondervan/Probe, 1978].)

bate ends in a stalemate. If the naturalist pushes his
arguments far enough to eliminate miracles, by implication he thereby eliminates the grounds for his own
beliefs. If he qualifies them so as to include all the
natural and scientific data he wishes, then he reopens
the door for miracles.

II. CHRYSSIDES' ARGUMENT AGAINST MIRACLES

A. *The Statement of the Argument*

One contemporary naturalist has formulated
another objection to miracles based on the repeatability principle.[61] George Chryssides, currently professor of philosophy at Plymouth Polytechnic in
Plymouth, England, has expounded his objection to
miracles in an interesting article. We may summarize
Chryssides' reasoning this way:

**Another
Naturalist
Argument**

1. No event can be attributed to a rational agent
   unless its occurrence is regular and repeatable.
2. Miracles are by nature not regular or repeatable.
3. Therefore, no miracle can be attributed to any
   rational agent (e.g., to God).

Technically, Chryssides is raising the problem of
the *identifiability* of miracles (which will be discussed
in chapter 5), but since his argument is based on the
unrepeatability of miracles, we will discuss this aspect here. The crucial premise in the argument is the
first one. It is based on the view that regularity or
repeatability is the only way to know that a given
event is caused by a rational agent. He writes, "My
argument will be that, *if* the concept of a violation of
scientific regularity makes sense . . . and *even
if*. . . . such a violation could be identified, it would
be logically impossible to ascribe such an event to the
activity of a rational agent."[62]

For example, argues Chryssides, "Suppose Jones
sees a mountain in the distance and says to the mountain, 'Mountain, cast yourself into the sea!', whereupon the mountain is observed to rise up from its

surroundings and fall into the water." If this occurred, "why should we say that Jones moved the mountain, rather than . . . by a strange coincidence the mountain happened to move . . . and fall into the water?"[63]

The crux of this argument is a premise (similar to the one offered by Hume) that a "necessary condition of the attribution of causality is . . . the *Repeatability Requirement*."[64] In short, a single instance cannot establish that there is a rational agent behind the event; it could simply be a "fluke." Only if one can perform the event on command over and over can he claim to be the rational cause of it.

Qualifications of Repeatability Principle

Chryssides acknowledges several qualifications of this repeatable principle. Repeatability does not imply (1) that we can predict the time of the event; (2) that the given event must occur many times (as long as similar events have occurred); (3) that the agent is capable of repeating the event (e.g., a lucky croquet shot); (4) that the antecedent conditions of the event can be specified by anyone in practice, but only in principle; (5) that the constant conjunction must be absolute (as Hume implied), but only that it must be regular; (6) that repeatability is a sufficient condition (since one could command a lighthouse to flash regularly without being the cause of the flashing).

Further, insists Chryssides, one must define an event in "such a way that its repetition is not logically impossible." What is necessary is to assert that "*similar* events will follow *similar* actions of human agents."[65] Or, to return to the example of Jones' "apparently moving the mountain, we may say that agency can be ascribed to Jones only if repetition of similar putative causes is accompanied by a repetition of similar putative effects. But if there is such regularity, this is statable in terms of scientific law, and if there is not, then agency cannot be ascribed."[66] In short, "a 'miracle' in this sense is logically impossible." For "the believer in miracles seems to wish to claim that the events he so describes are both caused and uncaused at the same time; they are caused, he says, in that they are due to the activity of an agent; they are uncaused, he says, in that they cannot be subsumed under scientific regularity. But he cannot have it both ways."[67]

B. *An Evaluation of the Argument*

Several points may be made in reply to Chryssides. First, his demands for determining rational agency seem too narrow. Repeatability isn't the only way to determine rationality, as even one of Chryssides' own illustrations would indicate. If dozens of people observe an amateur golfer hit a hole-in-one, they know the feat was caused by a rational agent, even though he cannot repeat it in practice (regularly). Furthermore, an event may be repeatable in principle, even though it is not actually repeated in practice. Not every song Handel wrote was a "Hallelujah Chorus," but would anyone deny that this song was a result of rational agency, even if he knows nothing about the composer? This unique work bears the unmistakable mark of intelligent authorship.

Second, regularity is not the only (or even the best) sign of rational agency; *adaptability* (or purposeful "fit") can also be a sign. All one needs to hear is a single clear SOS signal over a ship radio during a storm to know that it was sent by a rational agent. Such a brief but intelligible message has purposeful "fit" in that context. Likewise, most scientists who are listening for radio signals from outer space would accept the reception of only one (or, at most, a few) intelligible messages as proof of extraterrestrial intelligent existence. In truth, repeatability is not as good an indication of rational agency as is *intelligibility*. If one meets an extraterrestrial being emerging from a space ship who speaks even one word in English (e.g., "hello"), he would no doubt conclude the word proceeded from a rational agent, for even one word in this context would be an indication of rational agency.

This leads to a third objection to Chryssides' view. Whether or not one attributes an event to a rational agent will depend largely on the *context*. For instance, if one sees the three letters *SOS* in the middle of his alphabet soup, he will *not* assume that a ship is in distress; whereas the same letters on a ship radio in a storm would be a sign of intelligent agents. Likewise, fire from the sky consuming an animal on an altar is not, *as such*, a proof that God did it. However, in the *context* of a theistic world and a prophet calling on God to vindicate Himself over false gods, it is a different matter! The crux of the matter as to whether God is the cause of an event will depend on the total *theistic-moral context* of the event.

Chryssides' Inconsistency

Fourth, Chryssides is inconsistent. He argues that a "miracle" is logically impossible and yet insists that a natural event has repeatability and *must* be defined in "such a way that its repetition is not logically impossible."[68] How can he rule out supernaturalism logically and yet insist that naturalism cannot be eliminated in the same way? But if the rules of the game are "heads the naturalist wins and tails the supernaturalist loses," then there is not much chance for a miracle, is there?

Fifth, Chryssides' position dies a death by qualification. By the time he finishes qualifying what repeatability means, the supernaturalist can claim similar theistic conditions for miracles. For he admits that the event need not be predictable in advance, repeated more than once, or have to specify its conditions in advance. Yet when God desires to perform other miracles, then like supernatural event follows from like supernatural cause (God).

The only real difference Chryssides can point to is one readily granted by the theist, namely, that natural events can occur *more often* than miracles. But this difference is not crucial to determining rational agency. For as long as miracles occur often enough to determine that they are not pure flukes and can be repeated, then Chryssides' criteria have been met. The real question, then, is not how regularly a "miracle" must occur to count as an act of God (Chryssides admits that *many* actual occurrences are unnecessary), but whether *any* miracles do indeed occur. And this possibility cannot be eliminated by philosophy (unless one can disprove the existence of God); rather, it is a matter of history (see chapter 11).

45

Are Miracles
Repeatable?

SUMMARY AND CONCLUSION

Both Flew and Chryssides developed Hume's principle of "constant conjunction" into a repeatability criterion for eliminating the miraculous (or at least a credible *knowledge* of it). Both, however, fail because they either beg the question by assuming naturalism is true, or else they destroy their position by qualification. In brief, if one takes a narrow definition of natural law, then, along with miracles, he eliminates some natural events, as well. And if one qualifies and broadens his definition of natural law, then he makes room for miracles too.

Summarizing the Critiques of Flew and Chryssides

Does not the fact that naturalists have found it necessary to change the definition of the natural indicate that their reasons for trying to eliminate miracles are not strictly scientific? Recently, in a very revealing admission, an Ivy League physics professor told me that his "reason" for accepting a naturalistic perspective was that "it is ethically more comfortable to believe this way." This, then, is not a matter of scientific fact but of life's *choice*.

The faith nature of the attempts to eliminate miracles becomes obvious when, in examining what naturalists have claimed would qualify as a miracle, we see the change from Hume to the present. Hume admitted that healings (and raising the dead) would be miracles.[69] He would admit that walking on water was miraculous, but Chryssides denied this. But the believer in the miraculous is tempted to ask, If walking on water, moving mountains on command, and raising the dead do not qualify as miracles, then what does qualify? It would seem that the naturalists are changing the rules in order to explain away miracles that they cannot easily deny have happened.

This point is forcefully made in the story of the psychotic patient who thought he was dead. Seemingly no empirical test (feeling, seeing, etc.) would convince him that he was alive, for he would claim that dead people can feel, see, etc. Finally, in desperation, the doctor asked him if dead men could bleed. "No," he replied. "Ah," said the doctor, who promptly punctured the patient's finger with a pin. Seeing the blood, the patient thereupon cried out, "My goodness, dead people do bleed!"

chapter four

Are Miracles Unscientific?

The modern contentions that miracles are contrary to scientific explanation and the scientific method are examined. The assumptions of such contentions and the logic of the arguments are also examined.

Modern life is largely a product of the scientific method. Automobiles, radios, TVs, jets, space exploration, satellites, and computers are all part of our way of life. Few show a serious willingness to leave all that our scientific civilization has provided and head for the raw jungle. It is for this reason that many are rejecting miracles. For they insist that the acceptance of the scientific method means the rejection of miracles.

So, in the wake of modern science it has been common for naturalists to attach their position to the scientific method. The result is that belief in miracles is held to be contrary to the scientific method. In short, miracles are held to be unscientific. This point has been argued several ways.

47

48

Miracles
and Modern
Thought

The
Nowell-Smith
Argument

I. Belief in Miracles Is Contrary to Scientific Explanation

A. *Statement of the Nowell-Smith Position*

Patrick Nowell-Smith has been professor of philosophy at York University in Toronto since 1969. Educated at Harvard and Oxford, he has taught previously at several universities, including the universities of Leicester and Kent in England.

In his famous essay "Miracles," Nowell-Smith objects to the supernaturalist's claim that an event is a miracle simply because it cannot be explained in terms of any scientific laws. He writes, "We may believe him [the supernaturalist] when he says that no scientific method or hypothesis known to him will explain it." But "to say that it is inexplicable as a result of natural agents is already beyond his competence as a scientist, and to say that it must be ascribed to supernatural agents is to say something that no one could possibly have the right to affirm on the evidence alone."[70] He argues that "no matter how strange an event someone reports, the statement that it must have been due to a supernatural agent cannot be a part of that report."[71] The reason for this rejection is clear. From the fact "that no scientist can at present explain certain phenomena," says Nowell-Smith, "it does not follow that the phenomena are inexplicable by scientific methods, still less that they must be attributed to supernatural agents."[72] That is, "there is still the possibility that science may be able, in the future, to offer an explanation which, though couched in quite new terms, remains strictly scientific."[73]

A good example of this is the fact that for many years it was held that bumblebee flight was unexplainable by natural law. However, the principles of this very natural occurrence have come to light in the discovery of power packs in the cells called mitochondria, which makes flight by rapid wing motion possible. This illustrates the folly of insisting that a presently unexplained event must be due to supernatural agents.

Just what is a *scientific* type of explanation? According to Nowell-Smith, "a scientific explanation is an hypothesis from which *predictions* can be made, which can afterwards be verified" (emphasis mine).[74] In addition, "an explanation must explain *how* an event comes about; otherwise it is simply a learned . . . name for the phenomenon to be explained." In view of this definition, "if miracles are 'lawful' it should be possible to state the laws; if not, the alleged explanation amounts to a confession that they are inexplicable." For "if we can detect any order in God's interventions it should be possible to extrapolate in the usual way and to predict when and how a miracle will occur. . . . otherwise the hypothesis is not open either to confirmation or refutation."[75]

Nowell-Smith concludes with this challenge to the supernaturalists:

> Let him consider the meaning of the word "explanation" and let him ask himself whether this notion does not involve that of a law or hypothesis capable of predictive expansion. And then let him ask himself whether such an explanation would not be natural, in whatever terms it was couched, and how the notion of "the supernatural" could play any part in it.[76]

Should the supernaturalist object that he is simply redefining the "natural" to include miracles, Nowell-Smith replies:

> I do not wish to quarrel about words. I will concede your supernatural, if this is all that it means. For the supernatural will be nothing but a new field for scientific inquiry, a field as different from physics as physics is from psychology, but not differing in principle or requiring any non-scientific method.[77]

We may now summarize the foregoing argument:

1. Only what has predictive capabilities can qualify as an explanation of an event.
2. A miracle cannot be predicted.
3. Therefore, a miracle does not qualify as an explanation of any event.

The long and short of this is that only *scientific* explanations can qualify as explanations, since only scientific explanations have predictive abilities. Hence, either miracles become scientific explanations or cease being explanations whatsoever. In brief, a miracle is *methodologically* unscientific. It is contrary to the scientific means of explaining events, a way that always involves the ability to predict similar events. Further, Nowell-Smith denies that rational agency is necessary to account for *any* anomaly of nature. Such aberrations will in time yield to application of scientific method. He says that all that happens will eventually be shown to result from natural law.

B. *An Evaluation of Nowell-Smith's Antisupernaturalism*

Despite the fact that he claims "the problem must be attacked with an open mind, that is to say, with a mind not disposed to reject evidence because it conflicts with some preconceived theory,"[78] Nowell-Smith evidences an invincible bias toward naturalism. For, in practice, any event in the world will ipso facto be declared by him a natural event. But if no event is ever permitted to have a miraculous interpretation, how can this be considered an "open-minded" view?

There are several indications that Nowell-Smith is really begging the question in favor of naturalism.

First of all, he defines "explanation" in such a narrow way as to eliminate the possibility of a supernatural explanation. Rather than being truly open to another kind of explanation than a natural one, he arbitrarily insists that all explanations must be *naturalistic* ones or else they do not really count as explanations.

The supernaturalist does not insist that "an event no matter how strange *must* have been due to a supernatural agent." It does seem likely that most strange events are natural, though as yet unaccounted for. The supernaturalist does object to Nowell-Smith's saying that supernatural agency "*cannot*" ever be part of the report of a strange event. The supernaturalist says that one should look at the alleged event to see if it was or was not a miracle. What the supernaturalist objects to is the naturalist's dogmatic assertion, before he even considers the evidence, that no miracle occurred.

Second, he simply assumes without proof that "all phenomena will *ultimately* admit of a natural explanation" (emphasis mine).[79] But how does he know this is so? Again, there is no empirical proof for this assumption. It is simply a matter of naturalistic faith! There is no factual proof given for it.

Third, even if he were presented with empirical evidence of a miracle, Nowell-Smith makes it very clear that he would *never* admit it is really a supernatural event. He will simply hope that some day, "ultimately," he will find a naturalistic explanation. Meanwhile, he will persist in *believing* that such an explanation can be found.

The Necessity of Predictive Value

Fourth, Nowell-Smith demands that all explanations must have predictive value to qualify as true explanations. And yet there are many natural events that no one can predict. One cannot predict if or when the town bachelor will marry. But when he does say, "I do," do we not claim that he was simply "doing what comes naturally"?

If the naturalist replies, as indeed he must, that he cannot always predict in practice (but only in principle) when natural events will occur, then the supernaturalist can do likewise. In principle we know that *a miracle will occur whenever God deems one necessary*. If we knew all the facts (which include the mind of God), then we could predict in practice precisely when this would be.

Fifth, Nowell-Smith shows the extent he is willing to go to exclude miracles as an explanation of some strange event. He begins by insisting that "the breakdown of *all* explanations in terms of present-day science does not . . . immediately force us outside the realm of the 'natural' " (emphasis mine).[80] The supernaturalist can (and does) agree with Nowell-Smith who admits "that the present hypotheses of science can never be expanded to cover miraculous phenomena." But the supernaturalist parts company with Nowell-Smith when he insists that "we may require new concepts and new laws.''[81] This insistence on ultimate natural causes for miracles is the essence of the naturalist mind. Such a position goes beyond what is warranted by the evidence. At this juncture, the naturalist demonstrates a faith commitment that rivals religious dedication.

Sixth, one of the problems behind this kind of scientific naturalism is the confusion of naturalistic *origin* and natural *function*. Motors function in accordance with physical laws but physical laws* do not produce motors; minds do. Likewise, a good poem functions in accordance with the laws of spelling and grammar. But these laws alone never produce a poem; only a mind can do that. In like manner, the origin of a miracle is not the physical and chemical laws of the universe, even though the resulting event will operate in accordance with these natural laws. In other words, a Virgin Birth (of divine origin) will produce a nine-month pregnancy (in accordance with natural law). So natural laws* do not produce things; they just govern the things that are produced.

II. MIRACLES ARE CONTRARY TO THE SCIENTIFIC METHOD

While Nowell-Smith pronounced miracles unscientific by virtue of their being contrary to scientific *explanation*, others have argued that miracles are contrary to the scientific *method*.

A. *The Charge That Miracles Are Contrary to Science as Science*

The McKinnon Argument

One proponent of this view, Alastair McKinnon, put the argument this way:

1. A scientific law is a generalization based on past observation.
2. Any exception to a scientific law invalidates that law as such and calls for a revision of it.
3. A miracle is an exception to a scientific law.

---

*Technically, the "law" does not *produce* or govern anything; it simply *describes* the process. It is the natural *force* that produces things, and the law describes the operation of this force.

4. Therefore, any so-called miracle would call for a revision of the present scientific law (and it would be assumed to be a natural event under any new law that explains it as a natural event). This means laws are like maps, and maps are never violated; they are only revised when they are found to be mistaken.

Even naturalists have admitted that this argument is easily refuted. As one put it, "This a priori argument can be refuted by noting that a supernaturally caused exception to a scientific law would *not* invalidate it, because scientific laws are designed to express *natural* regularities," and in the case of a miracle we have "a special and non-repeatable"[82] exception. That is to say, one nonrepeatable exception does not call for the revision of a natural law. More likely it would be credited to faulty observation, anyway. From a strictly scientific point of view a nonrepeatable exception is an anomaly. Scientists suspect lawful behavior in these anomalies if, under specified conditions, the anomaly recurs. In this case, anomalies would be pointers to the development of a more general natural law.

The development of quantum physics is a case in point. In certain experiments, matter behaved in a way that violated the laws of Newtonian physics. These instances were not miracles; they were indications that those Newtonian laws were not always correct. Miracles, however, do not come from random physical behavior patterns. They are occurrences that were *caused* to happen by the willful actions of rational agents (God or His representatives). That action of will is what cannot be repeated and therefore places miracles outside the realm of scientific observation. In other words, when a miracle takes place, it is because God wants it to, and one cannot arrange for God to "want to" cause one again simply so that we can watch. Miracles do not change our view of scientific laws, as quantum physics did; they simply step outside of them.

As has been observed, scientists and philosophers

are really interested only in *repeatable* exceptions to known laws. Hence, miracles would leave natural laws intact and therefore they would not be unscientific. Ninian Smart wrote, "Miracles are not experimental, repeatable. They are particular, peculiar events. . . . They are not small-scale laws. Consequently they do not destroy large-scale laws . . .; they have not the genuine deadly power of the negative instance."[83]

B. *Diamond's Argument That Miracles Would Destroy Science*

Diamond's Antisupernatural Argument

Others have attempted to salvage the argument against miracles from its alleged opposition to scientific methodology. For example, Malcolm Diamond, professor of philosophy at Princeton University, insists that it is disastrous to accept miraculous exceptions to scientific laws. For if one does accept some exceptions as supernatural, then "scientific development would either be stopped or else made completely capricious, because it would necessarily be a matter of whim or whether one invoked the concept of miracle."[84] In short, Diamond sees two problems with supernaturalism: (1) exceptions should not stop scientific research (they are in fact goads to further research) and (2) exceptions should not necessarily be called miracles. Does the odd always prove God? If not, then how does one distinguish the unusual from the supernatural?

According to Diamond, "Allowing for the possibility of supernatural explanations of naturally observable occurrences is something that would, in effect, drive working scientists to opt right out of the scientific enterprise." Why? "Because," insists Diamond, "these scientists would not be able to investigate [the miracle]. . . . As scientists they would not be able to determine whether the exception was supernatural."[85] In short,

scientists, as scientists, must operate with autonomy, that is, they must set their own rules and referee their own games. Therefore, although nothing logically would prevent a scientist from accepting the supernatural interpre-

So, says Diamond, "the answer that I shall offer on behalf of the naturalistic interpretation is pragmatic. It recommends reliance on the scientific explanations without pretending to be a conclusive refutation of supernaturalism."[87]

The outline of this argument is now clear. It is a pragmatic argument based on belief in the autonomy of the scientific method, which can be formulated thus:

1. Scientists, as scientists, cannot give up looking for naturalistic explanations for every event.
2. To admit even one miracle is to give up looking for a natural explanation.
3. Therefore, to admit miracles is to give up the scientific method.

C. An Evaluation of Diamond's Charge That Belief in Miracles Is Not in Accord With Scientific Method

We are now in a position to evaluate the charge that belief in miracles is unscientific. Diamond's comments make it clear that the basic assumption is the absolute autonomy of the scientific method. It is assumed as a matter of *faith* (with only *pragmatic* justification) that the scientific method is *the* method for determining all truth. Indeed, it is not just the scientific method but *one aspect* of the scientific approach (namely, the search for natural causes) that is assumed to be *the* only approach to truth. The following criticisms, then, may be offered against Diamond's arguments.

First, it is wrong, as Diamond implies, to presuppose that the scientific method necessarily entails naturalism. Scientists *as scientists* need not be so narrow as to believe, in advance of looking at every event, that nothing can ever count as a miracle. All a scientist need hold is that "every event has a cause" and that the "observable universe operates in an orderly way." To add that "every event has a *natural*

**Evaluating
the "Unscientific"
Charge**

cause" and "the observable universe operates in an absolutely *uniform* orderly way" is to load the scientific method with naturalistic presuppositions.

Second, as was pointed out, natural laws do not account for the *origin* of all events any more than the laws of physics alone explain the origin of a motor, or than the laws of grammar alone can account for a poem. Using a similar line of reasoning the former atheistic astronomer Sir Fred Hoyle and his Buddhist colleague, Dr. Wickramasignhe, have just concluded that there must have been a creator of life on earth. To their own surprise they calculated the odds against life arising by purely natural laws at $10^{40,000}$. This they said is as absurd as believing that a Boeing 747 can be produced by a tornado raging through a junk yard![88]

Third, it is *not* scientific to be closed-minded to reasonable explanations. And if there is a God who caused the universe to exist and who cares for it, then it is not unreasonable to expect that He can perform some regular activities (natural "laws") and also some special events ("miracles"). The only way to effectively disprove this possibility is to *disprove* that God exists, but most atheists agree that this is, strictly speaking, not possible to do.[89] Conversely, if God exists, then miracles are possible. The truly scientific and open mind will not dismiss in advance, logically or methodologically, the possibility of identifying some miraculous events. It will not presuppose, as Diamond does, that "the scientists, as scientists, *must* operate with [naturalistic] autonomy" (emphasis mine).[90]

Fourth, even if one grants that the scientific method can describe *how* an event occurred, this does not mean that the event cannot be miraculous. For instance, the fact that the Bible says the Red Sea was driven back by a strong east wind (Exod. 14:21) does not mean that the event was not miraculous. The miraculous element could be in *why* it happened *when* it happened, not simply in *how* it happened. Sometimes the miraculousness may be more in *teleology* (purpose) and *timing* than in the tools or means used to accomplish it. As long as the event is naturally *unusual* and theologically *purposeful*, it can qualify as a miracle, even *if* the immediate process is scientifically explainable. And the fact that outside intelligence with tremendous power can perform (or repeat) an unusual feat does not mean that God is ruled out. After all, an *unusual intervention by a powerful outside intelligence* (God) is precisely what is involved in a miracle.*

Fifth, when one reduces the argument against miracles to its basic premise it amounts to this:

1. Whatever actually occurs in the natural world is a natural event.
2. Some so-called miracles have actually occurred.
3. Therefore, these so-called miracles are really natural events.

Now the circular nature of the naturalist's argument is laid bare. *Whatever happens in the natural world is, ipso facto, a natural event!* The fallacy is obvious: whatever occurs *in* nature was caused *by* nature. This, of course, assumes what is to be proven; namely, there is no supernatural being (God) who can act in nature. Just because an event occurs in the world does not mean it was caused by the world. It may have been specially caused by the God beyond the world.

D. *The Integrity of the Scientific Method*

There is yet one implication of the methodological critique that has not been addressed: If miracles are allowed, how can one retain the integrity of the scientific method? If some events are ruled out of bounds to the scientists, then has not the supernaturalist closed the door to rational examination of some events? Or, even more to the point, once one allows miracles, how can there be a meaningfully definable role for scientific exploration?

---

*This raises the question of precisely how one can identify an unusual event as an act of God. This matter will be discussed in chapter 11.

58

Miracles
and Modern
Thought

Miracles
and
Method

In response to this legitimate inquiry, several things should be noted. First, the belief in miracles does not destroy the *integrity* of scientific methodology, only its *sovereignty*. It says in effect that science does not have sovereign claim to explain all events as natural, but only those that are regular, repeatable, and/or predictable. Scientific law, does not include anomalies, for by its very nature an anomaly (no law) has no law covering it. And to assume that all anomalies do have unknown covering laws is to beg the question in favor of naturalism. Science *as science* must not assume this, since it has no *scientific* grounds for such an assumption. The only scientific grounds for doing so would be that the event could be repeated and/or predicted (and in the case of a miracle, it cannot).

Second, science has a right to expect that natural laws (i.e., natural forces) will govern the *function* of the world. But science has no right to demand that these same natural laws can account for the *origin* of every event in the world. For while natural laws can explain the erosion in the badlands, they do not account for the presidents' faces on Mount Rushmore! Only intelligent intervention from the outside explains the faces. So the integrity of science can be maintained over world processes without giving it the exclusive rights to explain the origin of all events in the world. When science demands that the *genesis* of all events must be natural, and not simply the *governance* of these events, then it has ceased being science; it has become philosophical naturalism.

Third, science is not sovereign over *all* events but only over all regular, repeatable, and/or predictable ones. Technically speaking, science need not be concerned with particular events as such, but only with types, classes, or kinds of events. Admitting that some events do not fall into these types does not destroy the types or classes.

Finally, science can be sovereign in describing *how* but not in explaining *why* an event occurs. And if an unusual occurrence shows signs of intelligent intervention (e.g., the faces of Mount Rushmore), then the scientist has no right to call it an anomaly of nature.

Science is unlimited in *classification* of events, but it is not unlimited in naturalistic *explanation* of events. That is, the scientist has a right—even an obligation—to examine all events. However, in all honesty *as a scientist*, he must place some events in the class of "not yet explainable as natural events." Of these, some may be supernatural, but simply to assume that all "not yet explained" events must thereby be naturally explainable goes far beyond science as such. It moves into a *philosophical* belief in naturalism.

SUMMARY AND CONCLUSION

Various attempts have been made by naturalists to prove that accepting miracles is *unscientific*. Some have insisted that believing in miracles is contrary to scientific explanations; others say it is contrary to scientific methodology. The first argue that miracles, contrary to natural laws, are unpredictable; others contend that miracles are unrepeatable or would sacrifice the autonomy of science. In each case, it has been shown that the arguments beg the question in favor of naturalism. That is, they *assume* the scientific method must be defined in such a way as to exclude the acceptance of miracles. In effect, they have insisted that, by its very nature, the scientific method dictates in advance that every event must be considered natural. The central but hidden premise is invincibly antisupernatural: "Every event in the world must be assumed to be a naturally caused event." If one does not now have a naturalistic explanation, then he must never give up believing that "ultimately" there is one. Of course, the supernaturalist cries, "Unfair!" He points out that one does not have to be incorrigibly naturalistic to be scientific.

Summarizing the Critiques of Antisupernaturalism

Contrary to the views of Nowell-Smith, miracles do not destroy the integrity of the scientific method. Science is possible as long as one assumes, as theists do, that the world is *orderly* and *regular* and that it operates in accordance with the law of *causality*. In point of fact, some noted modern philosophers such as A. N. Whitehead (in *Science and the Modern*

World) have observed that Christianity is really the mother of science.[91] And the contemporary philosopher-scientist Ian Barbour claims (in *Science and Religion*) that it was specifically the Christian belief in creation that gave much of the impetus for modern science.[92]

Furthermore, simply because most events are regular and predictable does not mean that *all* are. Nor does the fact that every event has a cause mean that every cause must be a *natural* one. The fact that science should be allowed a rational examination (and classification) of all events does not mean that it must give a naturalistic explanation of them. If the evidence does not support a natural explanation of the event, then the scientific approach should not rule out the possibility of a miracle.

chapter five

Are Miracles
Identifiable?

The naturalist's position opposing the identifiability of miracles is critiqued. Then two theistic options are examined, both of which consider whether miracles can be identified.

Some contemporary naturalists have argued that miracles are not identifiable. If this position were true, it would have serious implications for traditional Christian beliefs. It would mean that no unique event from the biblical stories of Moses and Elijah to the resurrection of Jesus could be identifiable as a miracle. Likewise, no unusual healing that might lay claim to being divine in origin could be considered a miracle. There are two aspects to this argument. First, miracles in general must be identifiable before a particular miracle can be identified. Second, one must be able to point to distinguishing marks in order to identify a specific event as a miracle. Although Antony Flew's arguments (discussed in chapter 3) include 61 both of these aspects, we will focus on the identifiability of miracles in this chapter. (Chapters 9 and 11 will treat the problem of the actual identification of the miraculous.)

I. Flew's Argument Against the Identifiability of Miracles

Epistemological Objections

The basic objection to miracles by contemporary naturalists is not ontological but epistemological. Miracles are not rejected because they are known *not* to have occurred, but because they are not (or cannot be) known to *have* occurred. Antony Flew's objection fits into this category.

A. *Miracles Are Parasitical to Nature*

Flew begins his discussion with this definition of miracles: "A miracle is something which would never have happened had nature, as it were, been left to its own devices."[93] He notes that the great Christian theist Thomas Aquinas demonstrated that miracles are not properly a violation of natural law. Aquinas wrote that "it is not against the principle of craftsmanship . . . if a craftsman effects a change in his product, even after he has given it its first form."[94] Not only is this *power* inherent in the idea of craftsmanship, but so is the *mind* of the craftsman. So too a miracle bears the unmistakable mark not only of power but of the divine mind. A miracle, then, is "a striking interposition of divine power by which the operations of the ordinary course of nature are overruled, suspended, or modified."[95]

Accepting these theistic definitions of miracles, Flew goes on to insist that "exceptions are logically dependent upon rules. Only insofar as it can be shown that there is an order does it begin to be possible to show that the order is occasionally overridden."[96] In brief, miracles to Flew are logically parasitical to natural law. Hence, a strong view of miracles is impossible without a strong view of the regularity of nature.

B. *The Improbability of Miracles*

Flew quotes historian R. M. Grant to the effect that "credulity in antiquity varied inversely with the health of science and directly with the vigor of religion."[97] In short, miracles are prima facie (self-evidently) improbable.

David Strauss, a radical biblical critic of the nineteenth century, was even more skeptical. He wrote, "We may summarily reject all miracles, prophecies, narratives of angels and demons, and the like, as simply impossible and irreconcilable with the known and universal laws which govern the course of events."[98] Is such skepticism justified? According to Flew, it is justified on a methodological basis.

C. *The Problem of the Identifiability of Miracles*

Flew claims to be willing to allow (in principle at least) for the possibility of miracles. However, in actual practice, he argues that there is a serious (if not insurmountable) problem; it is the problem of *identifying* a miracle.

1. *First statement of Flew's argument*. The argument against miracles from their unidentifiability may be stated as follows:

1. A miracle must be identifiable (distinguishable) before it can be known to have occurred.
2. There are only two ways to identify (distinguish) a miracle: in terms of nature or in terms of the supernatural.
3. But to identify it by reference to the supernatural (as an act of God) begs the question.
4. And to identify it in reference to the natural event robs it of its supernaturalness.
5. Therefore, miracles cannot be known to have occurred, since there is no way to identify them.

Flew insists, against Augustine,[99] that if a miracle is merely "a portent [which] is not contrary to nature, but contrary to our knowledge of nature,"[100] then it

Are Miracles Identifiable?

Are Miracles Improbable?

Are Miracles Identifiable?

has no real apologetic value. For, argues Flew, if a miracle is merely a relativistic event *to us at present*, then it provides no proof that a revelation it alleges to support is *really* true. That is to say, whereas Augustine's notion of a miracle would assure the dependence of creation on God, it would do so only at the cost of subverting the apologetic value of miracles.[101] For if a miracle is not really contrary to nature, but only to our *knowledge* of nature, then a miracle is after all nothing but a natural event. In any event, we could not know that a miracle has *really* occurred, but only that it *seems* to us that one did.

Flew's point can be stated another way. In order to identify a miracle within nature, the identification of that miracle must be independent of nature. But there is no way to identify a miracle independently of the system by appealing to a supernatural realm; this would beg the question. It would argue in effect: "I know this is a miraculous event in the natural world because I know (on some independent basis) that it is supernaturally caused." And yet there is no natural way to identify a miracle. For unless it is already known (on independent grounds) that the event is miraculous, then it must be considered to be just another natural event. From the scientific point of view, it is just "odd" or inconsistent with previously known events. Such an event should not occasion worship but should simply stimulate *research* to find broader scientific law that could include it.

From this it would follow, argues Flew, that no alleged miraculous event can be used to prove that a religious system is true. That is to say, miracles can have no apologetic value. One cannot argue that God exists because an event is an act of God. For unless there is already a God who can act, there cannot be an act of God. In short, either the alleged miraculous event is known to be such because it is part of a supernatural system (which begs the question) or else one must be able to identify the event as supernatural from a strictly naturalistic perspective. But according to Flew, this is impossible, since an unusual event in the natural realm is, from a strictly naturalistic perspective, a strictly natural event.

heart of Flew's argument now comes into focus.[102]
Miracles are not identifiable, because there is no way
to define them. The reasoning proceeds thus:

1. A miracle must be identifiable before it can
   be identified.
2. A miracle can only be identified in one of two
   ways: either as
   a. an unusual event in nature, or
   b. an exception to nature.
3. But an unusual event in nature is simply a
   natural event, not a miracle.
4. And an exception to nature cannot be know
   (i.e., identified) from within nature.
5. Therefore, a miracle is not identifiable.

It would seem that Flew has made a penetrating
point. His first premise is solid: one must know what
he is looking for before he can ever know he has
found it. If he cannot define it, then he cannot be sure
he has discovered it. Likewise, the second point
exhausts the only two possibilities: it is either natural
or not natural. The strength of the third premise is
often missed by theists, especially those who work
out of a purely historical perspective. Unusual events
within nature are, as such, merely unusual events
within nature. Finally, the fourth point is well taken.

Actually, Flew's point can be strengthened: *How
can one know that an event is an act of God (miracle)
unless he already knows there is a God who can act?*
Unusual events—no matter how unusual they are—
are not and cannot ever be miracles unless there is a
God. And one cannot prove the existence of God from
an unusual event alone. That would beg the whole
question. For the existence of God is the necessary
presupposition of the event being a miracle. So then,
the unusual event cannot be used to prove what must
be presupposed in order for it to be a miracle. Therefore, unless the supernaturalist can support his belief
in God on some ground that is *independent of the
miracle*, he cannot know (identify) that it is a miracle.
Even the supernaturalist who does not use miracles to
prove God must first posit God before he can define a

miracle. And miracles must be definable or identifiable before one can be identified. Hence it would seem that Flew has shown, first, that miracles can never be used to prove God exists and, second, that miracles cannot even be identified, unless one first postulates God's existence.

II. A RESPONSE TO FLEW'S CRITIQUE

There are a number of ways that theists can respond to Flew's challenges. Some of them seem less fruitful and others appear to be futile, but there are some adequate responses.

A. *An Inadequate Response*

Some supernaturalists have argued that particular miracles (such as the resurrection of Christ) are so unusual that a divine cause is the only adequate explanation. John W. Montgomery, for example, contends that "the problem of 'miracles' . . . must be solved in the realm of historical investigation, not in the realm of philosophical speculation."[103] Why? Because "the resurrection argument has the . . . advantage of being . . . the fundament on which, ultimately, all other defenses rest."[104]

Just how does the miraculous provide this ultimate apologetic basis—even for proving that God exists? That is, how would Montgomery respond to Flew's argument? In his own words, "The problem here points to the question of the miraculous, and therefore I would like something bizarre in order to keep the aspect of miracle in view."[105] That is, the resurrection is so bizzarre, so odd, that only a supernatural explanation will adequately account for it. In more scientific terms, Montgomery thinks that the means by which one arrives at God from the resurrection is adductive, an extrapolation from the unusual. The conclusion "Christ is God" is obviously not a logical deduction from the premises (1) "I am God" and (2) "He rose from the dead." However, Montgomery insists that within the context of those claims, the deity of Christ is the most reasonable conclusion (extrapolation) that we can make from all the facts.

The problem is that this argument does not answer

Flew's objection. For unless one already knows (on independent grounds) that God exists, then no historical event can be justifiably identified as an act of God. The odd as such never leads to God. The odd doesn't prove God; it simply proves the odd. (Actually, it would be odd for anyone to think otherwise.) Of course, if one already grants (for whatever reason) that God actually exists, then the oddness of an event may very well be a clue (though not the only one) to its supernaturalness. But simply because an event is highly improbable does not mean it is miraculous— even if it has highly improbable truth claims connected with it.

There are many very unusual natural events that have happened. The odds for getting a perfect bridge hand are 1 in 1,635,013,559,600. But it has happened —naturally! Now the argument from the odd to God amounts to saying that *adding more zeros on the end of a probability ratio can transform an unusual event into a miracle*! On the contrary, it is an incontrovertible fact that if God does not exist, then, no matter what the odds against an event happening, it cannot be a miracle.* Likewise, unless one already posits God on other grounds, no odd event as such can count as a miracle. In fact, as Flew argued, it cannot even be defined as a miracle without reference to God.†

B. *A More Adequate Response*

In view of these naturalistic critiques, supernaturalists have two basic avenues of response. First,

---

*In a naturalistic world view, every event is seen through naturalistic "glasses." See my *Christian Apologetics* (Grand Rapids: Baker, 1976), chap. 15.

†Some may contend that if one cannot argue from a given event within the world (claimed as miraculous) to God, then neither can one argue from all the events of the universe to their cause (God), such as will be done below. Our response is that the cases are different. Apart from an already given theistic context, the analysis of no single event demands an infinite intelligent cause beyond the universe, for a particular event can always be explained in terms of some other event or of the whole universe. However, if the *whole* universe does not explain itself (i.e., if it is not uncaused), then it is necessary to posit a cause beyond it to explain it. Hence, the two situations are radically different.

they can assert that they have the same right as the naturalists simply to believe their view is true and to make God's existence a *presuppositional* prerequisite to miracles. Second, theists may offer some *rational* argument for the existence of God that is not based on an appeal to the miraculous.

The Presuppositionalist View

1. *Presupposing the existence of God*. Theists may respond to Flew by noting that the basis of naturalism is really *faith*—faith that there is a natural explanation to every event, even though they do not presently possess such an explanation. Many philosophers frankly admit that everything has first principles and that first principles cannot be proved. Stated another way, one must start somewhere, and starting points cannot be rationally proved. Theists may argue that just as the belief that all can be explained naturally is a faith commitment—without full proof—for the naturalists, so too theists may be permitted the same privilege. That is, theists may simply believe—without full proof—that there is a theistic explanation to the events of the world, some of them being unusual interventions of God called "miracles."

On this view, theists do not need to give a rational justification for their ultimate belief but simply a coherent explanation. This can be done by defining precisely what is meant by a miracle (see chapter 9), just as naturalists must define what is meant by a natural law. (Theists may not simply claim that everything unusual is a miracle, nor naturalists that everything is natural.) Hence, theists may begin looking for an event that they can identify as a miracle by presupposing that there is a supernatural realm in terms of which they can make their actual identification.

Some theists are content to take this approach. They point out that not only do naturalists beg the question by arguing in a circle, but *so do theists in their attempts*! In fact, they insist that all reasoning is circular.[106] For in the final analysis, they say, all thought is grounded in faith. Although this writer does not personally hold this position, it appears that, if they choose to go this route, their grounds (or lack of grounds) are just as good as those of the naturalists. Certainly the naturalists who attempt to rule out miracles on the basis of a faith commitment to naturalism are in no position to forbid theists from simply believing that God exists and, hence, that miracles are possible and identifiable. Once the naturalists are granted the privilege of a belief basis for naturalism, for which they have no rational or scientific proof, then in all fairness we must allow other alternate world views the same opportunity.

There is, however, another avenue of approach open to theists; they may offer some rational justification for their belief in God. If they are successful, then they can define (show the identifiability of) miracles in terms of the supernatural realm that they have *reason* to believe in. The following is offered as an example of such an approach.

2. *Offering a rational justification for God's existence*. By rational justification is meant a sound argument. Sound arguments are made up of only true premises from which a valid conclusion is drawn. The following premises of the argument are all apparently true. How they are known to be true and with what degree of certainty is unimportant here as long as it is reasonable to believe they are true. It is noteworthy to point out, however, that even nontheists generally hold them to be true. These premises are as follows:

1. Something exists.
2. Nothing cannot cause something; only something can cause something.
3. The effect resembles its cause in some significant way(s).

All of these premises are accepted as true by most people without serious question. The first one is undeniably true, since one cannot consistently deny that everything exists including oneself. One must exist before one can deny that anything exists. The second and third premises are obviously true as well. The popular song "Nothing comes from nothing; nothing ever could'' reflects the widespread belief in the truth of this statement. Even the skeptic David Hume wrote, ''I never asserted so absurd a proposition as that anything might arise without a cause.''[107] It seems obvious enough that absolutely nothing has absolutely no power to cause anything. It is a fundamental presupposition of scientific exploration that ''every event has a cause.''

The third premise is also an almost universally accepted truth. The popular adage ''Water can rise no higher then its source'' is evidence of the widely accepted truth that effects resemble their causes in some significant ways. To be sure there are accidental ways that effects do not resemble causes. Computers do not bear a physical resemblance to their inventors. However, their physical shape is not a significant or essential part of their intended purpose and function. But it is part of their true purpose and function to think and accomplish programmed work, and in this respect they do resemble their creators.

**Cause and
Effect**

Likewise, it is not legitimate to point to a student's exam and say that it bears no significant resemblance to the pen that produced those marks on the paper. For there is only an accidental relationship between the pen (only an instrumental cause of the exam) and the exam. However, there is an essential relationship between the student's mind (the efficient cause of the exam) and the exam. It is in this latter sense that every effect resembles its efficient cause. For instance, malaria does not resemble mosquitoes, since mosquitoes are not the cause but only the carrier. However, malaria parasites do resemble malaria parasites in significant and essential ways, because they are the cause of other parasites that resemble them. Likewise, musicians give birth to nonmusicians; but this special ability is only accidental to their humanity. But humans give birth to humans; that is an essential similarity.

Now granting that these premises are true—and it is certainly reasonable to believe that they are—then all that remains is to put them together in a valid way for the resulting argument to be a sound one. That is, a valid conclusion from true premises will yield a true conclusion. The following is a widely held theistic argument based on these three premises.

If something exists and if nothing cannot cause something, then it follows that something must necessarily and eternally exist. It must eternally exist since, if nothing ever was, then nothing could now be. But something undeniably now is. Therefore, something always has been. Likewise, something *must* always have been because nothing not only *does not* but *cannot* cause something. But if something is and if nothing cannot cause something, then it follows that something must *necessarily* always have been. Again, if something had not necessarily always have been, then nothing could now be, since nothing cannot bring something to be. Furthermore, this necessary and eternal being (which cannot come to be but must always be) must be the cause of everything that does come to be. For nothing cannot be the cause of what comes to be. Nor can something cause itself to come into being. For a cause is ontologically prior to its effect, and something cannot be prior to itself. It cannot exist prior to its coming into existence. Hence, only this necessary and eternal being can be the cause of whatever comes to be.

Now the space-time world (the cosmos, the universe) as conceived by modern scientists is obviously not an eternal and necessary being. Scientists tell us that the universe is not eternal, since it is subject to the second law of thermodynamics and is running down.[108] But whatever is running down must have been "wound up." That is, if the universe is running out of usable energy, then it must have had a beginning; otherwise it would have completely run out by now. Something with a fixed amount of energy does not take an eternity to run out of a fixed amount of energy.

Not is it plausible to believe that the universe is completely "rewinding" itself, for several reasons. First, it takes the creation of fresh hydrogen atoms to effect the rewinding, and it takes something to create the new atoms (nothing cannot make something).

Furthermore, even if the universe were "rebounding" again and again, nevertheless, like everything else subject to the second law, it too would not be rebounding as far each time and would eventually run down anyway. It would just take longer to do it.

Philosophic Objections to Eternal Cosmos

There are also philosophical reasons to believe that the space-time world is not eternal. The space-time world is made up of moments and events. But it is impossible to have an infinite number of moments or events. Mathematical or *abstract* infinites are possible, such as an infinite number of abstract points from, say, one end of your book shelf to the other. But one cannot have an infinite number of *actual* books on a book shelf no matter how long the shelf is. For no matter how long the shelf is, one could always make it a little longer.[109]

To change the illustration, no matter how long an actual chain is, one can always add one more link. Therefore, adding up finite moments will never reach eternity. So, no matter how far one carries back the moments of time, he will never reach the eternal. Time must have a beginning. And if space and time are a continuum wherein one is not found without the other, then neither can space be actually infinite. Abstract or conceptual infinites are possible but concrete and actual ones are not. But, as was already shown, there is an eternal and necessary existence. Thus the space-time world cannot be that eternal and necessary existence.

Some have tried to avoid this conclusion by insisting that the space-time world is "more" than a series of moments and events. Each part of the world is caused, they say, but the "whole" is more than the parts. In this way they hope to show that the universe, in the broader sense of the "whole," is uncaused, but the parts (events and moments) are caused.[110] Of course, if this is the case, then nontheists have just admitted what theists have been arguing for, namely, an uncaused, eternal and necessary existence that is more than the sum total of what is in the space-time universe. All that remains is to find out whether this uncaused eternal being is intelligent and moral. If it is intelligent and moral, then we have arrived at what theists mean by God.

This last step may be accomplished by using the third true premise from above: the effect must resemble its cause in some significant or essential way(s). Part of the space-time universe includes man who is an intelligent and moral being. Man is undeniably intelligent, for it takes an act of intelligence to formulate a denial of the truth of this claim. But if it takes intelligence to deny intelligence, then intelligence is actually undeniable.

Likewise, man is a value-oriented being. He uses and implies "oughts" or prescriptions. Even humanists believe in values and often strongly affirm them.[111] Indeed, it seems actually impossible to deny all value. For the one who formulates a denial, and so states it, implies thereby the value of so expressing himself. In more popular expression, those who deny the value of freedom are thereby enjoying the value of freedom of expression in their very denial.

Man a Value-oriented Being

Now if there is undeniably a being with the significant traits of intelligence and morality, and if the effect must resemble its cause in significant ways, then surely it is not unreasonable to conclude that this uncaused, eternal, and necessary being is also intelligent and moral. In popular language, if "water can rise no higher than its source," then it is surely reasonable to believe that it took a personal being (God) to make personal beings (human beings).

Certainly, if modern scientists succeed in making a computer robot that is genuinely and significantly personal, it will show that it took personal and intelligent beings (scientists) to make these personal and intelligent beings. One doubts seriously that the scientist who would succeed in doing this would turn down the Nobel prize on the grounds that it was not he but blind force or chance that deserves the honor! Surely that would be unreasonable. If so, then it is reasonable to believe, as theists do, that it was a personal, intelligent, and moral being who made this world.

Now the result of this argument can be assessed in different ways. For many theists it is a convincing argument for the existence of God. At the very least, it is an attempt to give a rational justification for God's existence, one that utilizes premises widely held to be true by both theists and nontheists. If it is in any way successful, then it provides the grounds for credible belief in the possibility of miracles. Or, to put it in terms of Flew's challenge, if it is reasonable to believe that God exists, then miracles are thereby identifiable. For if there is a supernatural realm (God), in terms of which a supernatural event can be defined, then a miraculous event is identifiable by reference to what is beyond nature. Of course, the fact that miracles are thus identifiable does not mean that one has thereby been identified. Before a person could identify a miracle, he would have to define a miracle and give evidence that some event actually fits the description. These problems will be discussed later.

SUMMARY AND CONCLUSION

**Summarizing
the Theistic
Response**

Naturalists, like Antony Flew, have argued that miracles cannot be known to have occurred unless they can first be defined or identified. But miracles cannot be identified unless they are identifiable. However, they cannot be identified from *within* nature. Hence supernaturalists seem to be in the vicious circle of postulating a supernatural realm as a ground for their belief in the supernatural.

To this theists may respond in two ways. First, like naturalists, whose system is ultimately built on a faith commitment, theists may simply postulate the existence of God as a faith commitment. Miracles, then, can be defined in terms of the characteristics of that God, as known from the Bible. From a strictly scientific point of view, miracles could be identified as anomalous events, but, since they are more than mere natural events, they could further be characterized by their moral and theological (Godlike) dimensions.

The other alternative open to theists is to offer independent (rational) grounds for believing in God and to use these characteristics of God to identify (define) miracles within the natural realm. In either event, the point of the naturalists is well taken. Miracles cannot be identified without a logically prior commitment (on whatever grounds) to the existence of God. One cannot know acts of God have occurred unless one postulates a God who can act. One can only discover God's "fingerprints" in the world if he posits a God whose "fingerprints" are known. But theists have just as much right simply to *believe* that the ultimate cause of these unusual Godlike events is supernatural as naturalists do to believe that ultimately there is a natural cause for all events, even though they do not know what it is. Indeed, rational theists are in an even better position, since they have provided rational grounds for their belief in the supernatural realm.

However, only on this latter approach can miracles have apologetic value. For only here is there a justification offered for believing in miracles. If one simply posits God without rational justification, he cannot validly use alleged miracles (acts of God) to prove the existence of God. For no matter how unusual an event is, it cannot be justifiably believed to be an act of God, unless there is some justification for believing that God exists apart from that event. On this point Flew seems to be right. But for theists who offer a rational justification for God, such as was done above, there is evidential value in miracles—at least to the degree that their argument for God is sound. But in any event—whether by proof or mere postulate of God—the theists can answer Flew's basic challenge of the identifiability of the miraculous by reference to the characteristics of a miracle (these characteristics will be discussed in chapter 9).

Are Miracles Mythological?

Rudolf Bultmann's assertion that the miracles of the New Testament are mythological and not historical is analyzed.

Traditional Christianity is firmly grounded in the miraculous, but not so with much of contemporary Christianity. Under attack from modern naturalism, many religious thinkers have denied that any events in the space-time world are miracles. Some have insisted that biblical miracles are myths. If this is so, then the heart of traditional Christian belief is false, since it is based on the belief in the bodily resurrection of Christ (see 1 Corinthians 15). Through a process of "demythologizing," some scholars insist the biblical records must be divested of their mythological "husk" to get at what is considered the existential "kernel" of truth. Rudolf Bultmann has been the foremost proponent of this new view of "miracles." 77

Bultmann (1884–1976) remains a key figure in modern religious and philosophical thought. A German theologian who pioneered the concept of "demythologizing" the Bible, Bultmann adapted phenomenologist Martin Heidegger's concept of "existential analysis" to New Testament exegesis. Using this methodology, Bultmann hoped "to separate the essential gospel message from the first-century world view."

I. BULTMANN'S DEMYTHOLOGICAL NATURALISM

A. *The Myth of a Three-Storied Universe*

**Rudolf
Bultmann's
Method**

Bultmann built his argument on several lines of argument. First, according to him, "the cosmology of the New Testament is essentially mythical in character." By this he means "the world is viewed as a three-storied structure, with the earth in the centre, the heaven above, and the underworld beneath." The world "is the scene of the supernatural activity of God and his angels on the one hand, and of Satan and his dæmons on the other. These supernatural forces intervene in the course of nature and in all that men think and will and do."[112]

B. *The Redemptive Myth*

**The Language
of "Myth"**

The New Testament, says Bultmann, presents its redemptive story in a miraculous, mythological form. "God sent forth his Son, a pre-existent divine Being, who appears on earth as a man. He dies the death of a sinner on the cross. . . . His resurrection marks the beginning of the cosmic catastrophe. . . . The risen Christ is exalted to the right hand of God in heaven and made 'Lord' and 'King.' "[113]

C. *The Obsolescence of the Mythological*

Rudolf Bultmann further considers that

all this is the language of mythology. . . . To this extent *the kerygma is incredible to modern man, for he is convinced that the mythical view of the world is obsolete*. [In view of this we] ask whether, when we preach the Gospel

to-day, we expect our converts to accept . . . the mythical view of the world in which it is set. If not does the
New Testament embody a truth which is quite independent of its mythical setting? If it does, theology must
undertake the task of stripping the Kerygma [proc-
lamation] from its mythical framework, of "demythologizing" it.[114]

Some Christians insist that modern men must accept the myth of the miraculous along with the message of the Gospel, but for Bultmann this would be
both senseless and impossible. "It would be senseless, because there is nothing specifically Christian in
the mythical view of the world as such. It is simply
the cosmology of a pre-scientific age." Further, "it
would be impossible, because no man can adopt a
view of the world by his own volition—it is already
determined for him by his place in history." The reason for this is that "all our thinking to-day is shaped
for good or ill by modern science." So "a blind acceptance of the New Testament mythology would be
irrational. . . . It would involve a sacrifice of the in-
tellect. . . . It would mean accepting a view of the
world in our faith and religion which we should deny
in our everyday life."[115]

D. *The Impossibility of the Miraculous*

With unlimited confidence, Bultmann pronounces
the biblical picture of miracles as impossible to modern man. For "man's knowledge and mastery of the
world have advanced to such an extent through science and technology that it is *no longer possible* for
anyone seriously to hold the New Testament view of
the world—in fact, there is hardly anyone who
does." Therefore, "the *only* honest way of reciting
the creeds is to strip the mythological framework from
the truth they enshrine. . . ." For "now that the
forces and the laws of nature have been discovered,
we can no longer believe in spirits, whether good or
evil."[116] It is simply "impossible to use electric light
and the wireless and to avail ourselves of modern
medical and surgical discoveries, and at the same time

to believe in the New Testament world of demons and spirits.''[117] Therefore, concludes Bultmann, "the *only relevant* . . . assumption is the view of the world which has been molded by modern science and the modern conception of human nature as a self-subsistent unity *immune from* the interference of supernatural powers" (emphasis mine).[118] This means that "*the resurrection of Jesus* is just as difficult, it means an event whereby a supernatural power is released. . . . To the biologists such language is meaningless. . . . such a notion [the idealist] finds *intolerable*.''[119]

E. *The Real Purpose of Myth*

If the biblical picture is mythological, how then are we to understand it? For Bultmann "the real purpose of myth is not to present an objective picture of the world as it is, but to express man's understanding of himself in the world in which he lives." Therefore, "myth should be interpreted not cosmologically, but anthropologically, or better still, existentially." That is, "myth speaks of the power or the powers which man supposes he experiences as the ground and limit of his world and of his own activity and suffering." In other words, "the real purpose of myth is to speak of a transcendent power which controls the world and man, but that purpose is impeded and obscured by the terms in which it is expressed.''[120]

Unlike the older liberal theologians who "used criticism to *eliminate* the mythology of the New Testament, our task to-day," wrote Bultmann, "is to use criticism to *interpret* it.''[121] How far does this criticism lead Bultmann? Was the Christ of the New Testament a mere mythical figure? Bultmann answers no. "He is also a concrete figure of history—Jesus of Nazareth. His life is more than a mythical event; it is a human life which ended in the tragedy of crucifixion. We have here a unique combination of history and myth.''[122] The miracles and resurrection of Christ, however, are another matter. They are not historical but suprahistorical events.

"Obviously [the resurrection] is not an event of past history. . . . An historical fact which involves a resurrection from the dead is utterly inconceivable."[123] Bultmann offers several reasons for his antisupernatural conclusion. First, there is "the incredibility of a mythical event like the resuscitation of a corpse—for that is what the resurrection means. . . ." Second, there is "the difficulty of establishing the objective historicity of the resurrection no matter how many witnesses are cited, as though once it was established it might be believed beyond all question and faith might have its unimpeachable guarantee." Third, "the resurrection is an article of faith. . . . So it cannot be a miraculous proof." Finally, "such a miracle is not otherwise unknown to mythology."[124]

In view of this, Bultmann says it is "abundantly clear that the New Testament is interested in the resurrection of Christ *simply and solely* because it is the eschatological event *par excellence*."[125] Hence, "if the event of Easter Day is in any sense an historical event additional to the event of the cross, it is *nothing else* than the rise of faith in the risen Lord. . . . *All* that historical criticism can establish is the fact that the first disciples came to believe in the resurrection" (emphasis mine).[126]

What then is the Resurrection, if it is not an event of space-time history? It is an event of subjective history, for "the historical problem is scarcely relevant to Christian belief in the Resurrection. For the historical event of the rise of the Easter faith means for us . . . the act of God in which the redemptive event of the cross is completed."[127] It is an event of subjective history, an event of faith in the hearts of the early disciples. As such, these "miracles" are not subject to objective historical verification or falsification, for they are not really events *in* the space-time world. Christ did not rise from Joseph's tomb, but He arose by faith in the disciples' hearts.

G. *Bultmann's Argument Restated*

It is obvious even to the casual reader that Bultmann is opposed to the miracles of the Bible, including even the resurrection of Christ. Before evaluating his conclusions, we will restate Bultmann's central claim.

A Naturalistic Base

In view of his rigid naturalistic presuppositions, it is not surprising that Bultmann engages in demythology of the Gospel record. What is of central importance here is his conclusion that "miracles" are by nature suprahistorical, that they are not events in the space-time world. It is difficult to formulate precisely what reasoning Bultmann uses to support this thesis. It seems to go like this:

1. Myths are by nature more than objective truths; they are transcendent truths of faith.
2. But what is not objective cannot be part of a verifiable space-time world.
3. Therefore, miracles (myths) are not part of the objective space-time world.

II. An Evaluation of Demythological Naturalism

A. *Critique of Bultmann's Position*

Critique of Bultmann's Naturalism

In view of the above summary of Bultmann's view of the miraculous, several objections can be offered.

First, it does not follow that because an event is *more* than objective and historical it must be *less* than historical. Gospel miracles, to be sure, have a "moreness" or transcendent dimension to them. They cannot be reduced to *mere* historical events. For example, the Virgin Birth is more than biological; it points to the divine nature of Christ and to the spiritual purpose of His mission. It is not merely a matter of science; it is also a "sign" (Isa. 7:14). The same is true of the Resurrection. It is *more* than a mere resuscitation of a corpse. It has a divine dimension that entails great spiritual truths as well (Rom. 4:25; 2 Tim. 1:10).

But having said all this, we are by no means bound to conclude that because these miracles are *more* than the purely objective and factual, they are not *at least* space-time events. Even Bultmann admits that the

New Testament writers believed these events to be
historical and so presented them: "It cannot be denied
that the resurrection of Jesus is often used in the New
Testament as a miraculous proof . . .: both the legend
of the empty tomb and the appearances insist on the
physical reality of the risen body of the Lord." However, Bultmann adds, "these are most certainly later
embellishments of the primitive tradition."[128] And
apart from simply presupposing the scientific "unac-
ceptability" of these miracles to "modern" man
(which we have already shown in chapter 4 to be a
false conclusion), there are no solid reasons for concluding that these events could not have occurred in
space-time history.

Second, to state the objection to Bultmann another
way, we could point out that simply because an event
is not *of* the world does not mean that it cannot occur
in the world. That is, a miracle can be *of* the supernatural world and yet it can occur *in* the natural
world. In this way the event can be objective and
verifiable without being reducible to purely factual
dimensions. Thus one could verify directly by historical means whether or not the corpse of Jesus of
Nazareth was resuscitated (the objective dimensions
of the miracle), without reducing the spiritual aspects
of the event to mere scientific data. But in claiming
that miracles such as the Resurrection *cannot* occur
in space-time history, Bultmann is merely revealing
his unjustified, dogmatic, naturalistic bias.

Third, it is evident that the basis of Bultmann's
antisupernaturalism is not evidential. It is something
he holds "no matter how many witnesses are
cited."[129] The dogmatism of his language is revealing. Miracles are "incredible," irrational," "no
longer possible," "meaningless," "utterly inconceivable," "simply impossible," and "intolerable."
Hence, the "only honest way" for modern men is to
hold that miracles are "nothing else than spiritual"
and that the physical world is "immune from interference" in a supernatural way. This is not the language
of one open to historical evidence for a miracle. It is a
mind that does not wish to be "confused" with the
facts!

**Existential
Treatment
of Miracles**

Finally, if miracles are not objective historical events, then they are unverifiable or unfalsifiable. That is, there is no factual way to determine their truth or falsity. But if this is so, then they have been placed beyond the realm of objective truth and must be treated as purely subjective and existential. If so, then Antony Flew's criticism is to the point when he writes:

> Now it often seems to people who are not religious as if there was no conceivable event or series of events the occurrence of which would be admitted by sophisticated religious people to be a sufficient reason for conceding "There wasn't a God after all." . . . What would have to occur or to have occurred to constitute for you a disproof of the love of, or of the existence of, God?[130]

To rephrase this for Bultmann, "If the corpse of Jesus of Nazareth had been discovered after the first Easter, would this falsify your belief in the Resurrection?" His answer is clearly no. By contrast the answer of the apostle Paul is clearly yes. For "if Christ has not been raised, your faith is worthless; you are still in your sins" (1 Cor. 15:17). Therefore, it is obvious that Bultmann's understanding of miracles is contrary to that found in one of the earliest Christian documents.*

Furthermore, if miracles are not historical events, then they have no evidential or apologetic value. Nothing can be *proved* by them since they have value only for those who wish to *believe* them. Again, this is not what the New Testament writers claimed for miracles. They considered them "convincing proofs" (Acts 1:3) and not "cleverly devised myths" (2 Peter 1:16 RSV).

SUMMARY AND CONCLUSION

**Summarizing
the Critique
of Bultmann**

Rudolf Bultmann faced the modern trend against miracles by insisting that miracles are mythological but not historical. They embody a spiritual truth (which must be demythologized from the legend).

---

*First Corinthians is acknowledged as a genuine Pauline letter by almost all New Testament scholars and is dated ca. A.D. 55.

However, this spiritual or existential truth is not a

space-time event. It is an event of faith. Christ, for example, did not rise from the tomb; He simply arose by faith in the disciples' hearts on the first Easter. In brief, miracles are not historical but suprahistorical. They are not events *in* the space-time world. Therefore, they cannot be objectively verified.

In response to Bultmann's assertions, four things have been pointed out. First, simply because miracles are more than historical does not mean they are *less* than historical. Second, miracles can be events *in* the world and yet not be *of* the world. Further, Bultmann's use of words such as "simply impossible" and "utterly inconceivable" shows that he is not really approaching the topic historically but dogmatically. Finally, Bultmann's view of objectively unverifiable and unfalsifiable.

Whether or not miracles have occurred in the world cannot be decided by philosophical dogma. It is a matter of historical research. But to say with Bultmann that miracles are purely suprahistorical myths not observable in the space-time world is not to accept traditional Judaism or Christianity. It is a vain attempt at reconciliation by capitulation.

chapter seven

Are Miracles Historical?

The arguments of the modern naturalist against the historical knowability of miracles are evaluated in the light of historiographic principles and logical construction.

In the last chapter we discussed the nature of biblical miracles. Are they mythical or historical? The conclusion was that, whatever else one may think of them, they claim to be historical, not suprahistorical, events. If this is the case, the question arises as to whether biblical miracles, as space-time events, are a proper subject of historical research. Some have argued that if the nature of miracles is understood to be historical, then the nature of the historical method renders miracles historically unknowable.

Again, it should be noted that serious implications rest in the balance here. First, if miracles are not historical, then the whole fabric of traditional Jewish and Christian belief is false. This means that traditional understanding of the story of Adam and Eve to the healings of Jesus is false. It also means that Christian belief at its heart is unverifiable from objective events either in the past or in the present and future. It means that Christianity is a subjective matter of belief but is not based on objective miraculous facts.

I. MIRACLE HISTORY IS UNKNOWABLE

A. *Troeltsch's Principles of Analogy*

Ernst Troeltsch and Historicism

Ernst Troeltsch was a German theologian of the liberal Protestant school. Born in 1865, he was educated in Germany and taught theology and philosophy at the University of Heidelberg from 1894 to 1914. Then he was professor of philosophy at the University of Berlin from 1915 until his death in 1923. Troeltsch is best known for his classical studies in historicism as historicism caused problems for religion since its inception during the Enlightenment. His involvement in an extensive study in historiography makes him especially significant in any historical study of miracles.

In his famous principles of historiography, Troeltsch laid down the rule of analogy: The only way one can know the past is by analogies in the present. The unknown is arrived at only through the known. In his own words, "on the analogy of the events known to us we seek by conjecture and sympathetic understanding to explain and reconstruct the past. . . ." Without uniformity of the present and the past, we could not know anything from the past. For without analogies from the present we cannot understand the past.[131]

On the basis of this principle, some have insisted that "no amount of testimony is ever permitted to establish as past reality a thing that cannot be found in present reality. . . ." Even if "the witness may have a perfect character—all that goes for nothing. . . ."[132] This would mean that, unless one can identify miracles (such as are found in the New Testament) in the present, we have no reason to believe that they occurred in the past, either. The English philosopher F. H. Bradley (1846–1924) stated the problem this way:

> We have seen that history rests in the last resort upon an inference from our experience, a judgment based upon

our own present state of things . . . ; when we are asked to affirm the existence in past time of events, the effects of causes which confessedly are without analogy in the world in which we live, and which we know—we are at a loss for any answer but this, that . . . we are asked to build a house without a foundation. . . . And how can we attempt this without contradicting ourselves?[133]

Now since it is widely admitted that no such miracles as virgin birth, walking on water, and raising the dead are occurring today, then it would follow (by Troeltsch's analogy) that such events cannot be known to have happened in history. In short, biblical miracles are historically unknowable.

B. *Flew's "Critical History"*

According to Antony Flew, "critical history" is based on two principles stated by David Hume.[134] Flew comments:

1. "The present detritus [remains] of the past cannot be interpreted as historical evidence at all, unless we presume that the same basic regularities obtained then as today.
2. "The historian must employ as criteria all his present knowledge, or presumed knowledge, of what is probable or improbable, possible or impossible."[135]

Now, writes Flew, "it is only and precisely by presuming that the laws that hold today held in the past . . . that we can rationally interpret the detritus of the past as evidence and from it construct our account of what actually happened."[136]

In the light of this discussion, Flew concludes (as noted in chapter 3) that "the critical historian, confronted with some story of a miracle, will usually dismiss it out of hand. . . ."[137] When asked "to justify his procedure, he will have to appeal to precisely the principle which Hume advanced: the 'absolute impossibility or miraculous nature' of the events attested must, 'in the eyes of all reasonable people . . . alone be regarded as a sufficient refutation.' "[138] This

Flew: The Historian Must Reject Miracles

impossibility, Flew adds quickly, is not logical but physical. Miracles are possible in principle, but in practice the historian must always reject them. For the very *nature* of the historical method demands that the past be interpreted in accordance with the (naturalistic) regularities of the present.

C. *Summary of the Historical Argument*

**Analysis of
Flew**

We may now summarize the premises of Flew's argument and begin to analyze it.

1. All critical history depends on the validity of two principles:
   a. The remains of the past can be used as evidence for reconstructing history only if we presume the same basic regularities of nature held then as now.
   b. The critical historian must use his present knowledge of the possible and probable as criteria for knowing the past.
2. But belief in miracles is contrary to both of these principles.
3. Therefore, belief in miracles is contrary to critical history.

Conversely, only the naïve and uncritical can believe in miracles. For the past can be known only in terms of the regular patterns of the present. And these patterns of nature in the present rule out any knowledge of miracles in the past.

II. AN EVALUATION OF THE HISTORICAL ARGUMENT AGAINST MIRACLES

A. *Some General Observations*

**Evaluating
the Historical
Argument**

It should be noted that this argument does not eliminate the *possibility* of miracles. It simply attempts to rule out their *knowability* by what Flew calls "critical history." Further, the argument (as Flew admits) follows the basic form of Hume's anti-supernaturalism (which has already been discussed in chapters 2 and 3). That is to say, it assumes that to be

truly critical and historical one must be antisupernatural. On the contrary, one would think that a truly
critical mind would not be closed to any possibility to
which the evidence actually pointed.

B. Specific Criticisms of the "Critical History" Approach

There are a number of fallacies involved in the above argument. Let us note several.

1. *Special pleading*. The first fallacy to note is that of special pleading. Flew is not willing to allow evidence to count for any *particular* events, such as miracles, in lieu of the evidence for events in general. That is, since there are far more regular and repeatable events than the special and unrepeatable kind (miracles), this fact is used to argue that the particular event counts as *no* real evidence at all. In effect, Flew is *adding* evidence for other like events, rather than *weighing* evidence for particular events. It is like refusing to believe that one has won the lottery, simply because there are thousands more who have lost!

Flew special pleads in another way. He assumes (without proof) that there are no miracles in the present. Maybe there are none. That is beside the point. He must *prove* there are none and not simply assume it. For if there are miracles in the present, then one would possess the needed analogy for knowing the past.

2. *Begging the question*. Flew commits the fallacy of *petitio principii*, for in practice he admits that miracles are "absolutely impossible" and that the critical thinker will dismiss them "out of hand." But why should a critical thinker be so biased against the historical actuality of a miracle? Why should he begin with a methodology loaded against certain kinds of events occurring in the past, before he ever looks at the evidence for them?

3. *Historical uniformitarianism*. Another way to state this objection is that Flew has adopted a historical uniformitarianism. He begins by *assuming* that all past events are uniformly the same as present ones.*

---

*There is a parallel here in the science of geology, which long overlooked the fact that many past processes were catastrophic and much faster than observed ones in the present.

This is not only a mere assumption, but it is contrary to the belief of these naturalistic scientists (and of most scientists) about origins. For scientists believe that the origin of the universe and the origin of life are singular and unrepeatable events. But if the past can be known only in terms of the processes of the present, then there would be no scientific basis for knowledge about these origins, since they are singular and unrepeatable events of the past. Such an assumption is harmful to scientific progress, as the next point will illustrate.

4. *A hindrance to scientific progress*. The following is a tragic illustration of the hindrance of uniformitarian views to the progress of science. As introduced in chapter 1, these hindering views have been evident in the thinking of some of the most brilliant minds of modern science. The astrophysicist, Robert Jastrow, wrote, "There is a kind of religion in science; it is the religion of a person who believes . . . every event can be explained in a rational way as the product of some previous event."[139] The problem with this, declared Jastrow, is that "this religious faith of the scientist" is being upset by his own scientific discoveries.

The
"Big Bang"
Theory
Criticized

The Big Bang theory of the origin of the universe is a case in point. As pointed out in chapter 1, Eddington spoke of this nonuniform, special, explosive beginning of the universe with a Big Bang as "repugnant," "preposterous," and "incredible."[140] The German chemist Walter Nernst wrote, "To deny the infinite duration of time [with a Big Bang beginning] would be to betray the very foundations of science."[141] After Einstein made his school boy's mistake in mathematics attempting to refute the Big Bang theory, he admitted it was because the evidence pointed to a conclusion he was uncomfortable with at the time. Elsewhere he added, "To admit such possibilities seems senseless."[142] But Einstein finally admitted his mathematical errors and recanted his rejection of the Big Bang theory in view of the overwhelming evidence and in view of his own theory of relativity.

In brief, the presupposition that the past operates with the same processes as the present is apparently false. The evidence that supports the Big Bang theory[143] shows that the process by which the universe came to be is unique. Many scientists believe that the basic hydrogen atoms of the universe were created in milliseconds. Most astronomers today believe the universe began with a great explosion (several billions of years ago). But there is nothing like this occurring in the present! Therefore, on Flew's basis, we would have to reject out of hand this modern scientific understanding of the universe, simply because we have no like events today.

5. *Appealing to the general to rule out the particular.* There is a strange sort of logic going on in Flew's argument. It amounts to claiming that one must judge all *particular* (special) events in the past on the basis of *general* (regular) events in the present. But why should one do this? Why not use special events in the present as an analogy for special events in the past?* There are unique and particular events in the present. Scientists call them anomalies. From a *strictly* scientific point of view a miracle is like an anomaly. Of course, miracles have other characteristics (theological and moral ones) that an anomaly does not. (See chapter 9.) But all one needs to do for a meaningful understanding of a past miracle (assuming none exist in the present) is to combine the anomalous with the moral-theological characteristics known of God and the result is an understanding of what is meant by a miracle.

**Flew's
Strange
Logic**

Along these same lines, the contemporary philosopher Douglas K. Erlandson argues that scientific law, as such, is concerned with *types* of events (i.e., with general classes of events), whereas the supernaturalist

---

*It is not our purpose here to develop a methodology for knowing miraculous events in the past. A sketch of the basic elements will suffice. A "miracle" is like an anomaly but with the theological and moral context appropriate to a theistic God. Or, in other words, a miracle can be defined by elements known to us in the present (see chapter 9). Hence, miracles of the past can be known in the present.

is concerned with *exceptions* (particular events that do not fit into general classes). And a belief in the latter does not upset a belief in the former.[144] To put this in Flew's terms, one can believe that the "basic regularities" of the present did indeed obtain in the past, without insisting there were absolutely no exceptions to these regular patterns (or types) in the past. Only when one oversteps the observation of and scientific basis for natural law and insists that the "regularities" were really absolute *uniformities* can the knowability of miracles be eliminated.

6. *It proves too much*. Another way to state the fallacy in Flew's reasoning is to note that his argument proves too much—it proves that much of what he and other naturalists believe about the past cannot be true. As Richard Whately showed in his famous satire on Hume's naturalistic skepticism (see chapter 2),[145] if one must reject unique events in the past because there is no analogy in the present, then he would have to conclude that the accepted history of Napoleon—with its incredible and unique military exploits—is untrue.

7. *It is not really critical enough*. Flew's approach to history is not really critical enough. It does not criticize the uncritical, unreasonable acceptance of presuppositions that eliminate valid historical knowledge. Far from being open to evidence, Flew's naturalism eliminates in advance any miraculous interpretation of events in the past. In effect, it *legislates* meaning rather than *looks* for it. He claims to know in advance what these past events *must* mean, rather than seeking to understand what they *do* mean.

Summary and Conclusion

Following principles of historical interpretation laid down by Hume and Troeltsch, some modern naturalists have argued that miracles are historically unknowable. This is so, they say, because the past can be known only in terms of the present, and the present operates in a regular (uniform) frame.

In response, it has been shown that this argument engages in special pleading and begging the question in favor of naturalism. Furthermore, if this historical uniformitarianism is accepted, it will hinder scientific progress such as has been manifest in recent understanding of the origin of the universe. In addition to this, one can maintain the regularity of the past and its similarity to the present and still admit to some (miraculous) exceptions to this regular pattern. Finally, contrary to the naturalistic historian, the truly "critical" mind should not legislate the meaning of past events; it should look for their true meaning— whether this is natural or supernatural.

The implication of this, then, is that Christian claims are historically verifiable. It is not simply a matter of subjective belief. One can examine the records of the past and, by rational means, determine whether certain Jewish or Christian claims are true or false.

chapter eight

Are Miracles
Essential?

*Thomas Hobbes contends that miracles are contrary to
reason, but he declares that faith in them is to be com-
mended. Kant finds them neither essential for faith nor
necessary for the essence of true religion. These cases are
reviewed in the light of biblical and logical argument.*

Even if miracles have occurred, many devoutly
religious people have denied that they are really essential to religion. Some of the great religious minds
in the modern world have followed this approach to
the miracles question. Their reasons provide a very
subtle but significant argument for naturalism.

Again, if these men are right, traditional Christianity and Judaism are wrong, since both used miracles as a support of the very heart of their belief (e.g.,
Dan. 2–7; Acts 1–2; 1 Cor. 15; Heb. 2:3–4).
Likewise, much of modern religious belief is mis-
directed with its emphasis on supernatural conver-
sions and miraculous prophecies about the future.

Indeed, if miracles are not essential to true religion,   97 one should be content with normal religious experience common to mankind. One should make no claim to unique divine confirmation of any religious experience as certain select groups do (e.g., evangelical, "born-again" Christianity). With this in mind we will turn now to two of the better-known thinkers who argued along naturalistic lines on the issue of miracles: Thomas Hobbes and Immanuel Kant.

I. Miracles Are Not Essential to True Religion

It will be remembered that Spinoza insisted that miracles were not only unhelpful to true religion but actually harmful to it. He declared that all that is essential to true religion is basically moral. The whole of the Protestant tradition following Friedrich Schleiermacher (1768–1834), the father of modern religious liberalism, adopted this basic stance as well.[146] Hobbes and Kant had also been early proponents of this view.

A. *Hobbes: Miracles Can Be Harmful to Religion*

**Hobbes'
Natural
Religion**

One of the major forces in early British empiricism, Hobbes (1588–1679) was a well-trained classicist and logician. His legacy to the history of philosophy resulted from his penchant for deductive reasoning, which he acquired following a perusal of Euclid's *Geometry*. Hobbes' deductive reasoning combined empirical and rationalistic methods in a naturalistic philosophical system. One of the ramifications of his system was a discussion of the "natural" religion that denies the supernatural; thus his importance for this study.

But Hobbes' "natural religion" was a much more subtle denunciation of miracles than was Spinoza's pantheism. In fact, his probable denial was cast in the form of a tongue-in-cheek "defense" of the Christian religion.

1. *Naturalistic explanation of non-Christian miracles*. According to Hobbes, the origin of natural religion is found in four things: "opinion of ghosts, ignorance of second causes, devotion towards what men fear, and taking of things casual for prognos-

when they do not know the natural causes. "For the
way by which they think these invisible agents
wrought their effects [is through] men that know not
what it is that we call *causing*. . . ."[148] If they knew
the natural cause, they would not attribute a supernatural one to it.

2. *Miracles are the basis for revealed religion*.
Probably with tongue in cheek, Hobbes claims the
situation is much better for the supernaturally revealed religion of Christianity. For "where God himself by supernatural revelation planted religion, there
he also made to himself a peculiar kingdom. . . ."
The basis of this kind of religion "can be no other
than the operation of miracles, or true prophecy
(which also is a miracle). . . ." Of course, he says
"that which taketh away the reputation of wisdom in
him that formeth a religion . . . is the enjoining of a
belief of contradictories . . . , and therefore to enjoin
the belief of them is an argument of ignorance. . . ."
Likewise, "that which taketh away the reputation of
sincerity is the doing or saying of such things as appear to be signs that what they require other men to
believe is not believed by themselves." All of this is
scandalous and along with the "injustice, cruelty,
profaneness, avarice, and luxury" of those who pro-
pound such miracles, there is a stumbling block of
those who would believe.[149]

3. *When miracles fail, faith falls*. Besides the serious doubts, both of natural and revealed religion, that
Hobbes casts on the belief in supernatural causes,
Hobbes offers a subtle argument against the useful-
ness of miracles. Noting the apostasy of the people in
biblical times after the great prophets (Moses, Elijah,
et al.) had performed their great miracles, Hobbes
adds, "So that Miracles failing, faith also failed."[150]
This is to say, miracles are not really that helpful after
all. For as soon as they disappear so does the faith
they aroused.

4. *Desupernaturalizing the gospel record*. On the
basis of his materialistic understanding of the world,

**Disappearing
Faith**

Hobbes engaged in some desupernaturalizing of the Gospel record. He boldly proclaims that "the Scriptures by the Spirit of God in man mean a man's spirit, inclined to godliness."[151] As to the story of Jesus casting a demon out of a man, Hobbes said, "I see nothing at all in the Scripture that requireth a belief that demoniacs were any other thing but madmen."[152]

Piety, Not Philosophy

5. *What is essential to religion?* For Hobbes, miracles are not essential and probably not even helpful to religion. What is essential to religion is faith. Claiming that "natural reason" is the "undoubted word of God," Hobbes insists that in the religious realm we must live by "the will of obedience" to the lawfully imposed religion of the state. This means that "we so speak as, by lawful authority, we are commanded; and when we live accordingly; which, in sum, is trust and faith reposed in him that speaketh [the ruler], though the mind be incapable of any notion at all from the words spoken."[153] In a word, faith and obedience are what is essential to religion, not reason. Piety, not philosophy, is all that God expects of believers. There is complete separation of faith and fact. Hence, belief in objective factual miracles is not essential to true religious faith.

B. *Kant: Miracles Are Incompatible With True Religion*

Immanuel Kant (1724-1804) is our second naturalistic philosopher who denied any value of miracles to religion. He was a German transcendentalist and metaphysician during the Enlightenment.

Kant's impact on the history of philosophy has been felt especially in the area of epistemology. According to him, one's ability to know God or any aspect of the supernatural (specifically miracles) is limited. In one sense, Kant's view on miracles is far more helpful to naturalism than is David Hume's. Hume's attack on supernaturalism is frontal but Kant's is subterranean; so this study of miracles must take it seriously.

1. *Morality is the essence of true religion.* For Kant morality is the heart of true religion. *Theoretical* reason can never reach God.[154] There is a gulf that cannot be spanned between the world *to us (phenomena)* and the world *in itself (noumena).* We can know appearance but not reality. Only by *practical* reason can God be known.[155] In fact, men must strive to live "within the limits of [practical] reason alone."[156] Foreshadowing Schleiermacher, Kant claimed that man must use this practical or moral reason to determine what is essential to religion. This moral reason should be a guide to interpreting the Bible. "Frequently this interpretation may, in the light of the text (of the revelation), appear forced—it may often really be forced; and yet if the text can possibly support it, it must be preferred to a literal interpretation. . . ."[157] In fact, the Bible's moral teaching "cannot but convince him of its divine nature. . . ."[158] In this moral law, then, is the essence of true religion, the Spirit of God.[159]

2. *Morality eliminates the need for miracles.* Using morality as the rule for religious truth, Kant concluded that miracles were merely an appropriate introduction to Christianity but not strictly necessary for it. In fact, he says, moral religion must "in the end render superfluous the belief in miracles in general." To believe that miracles can be helpful to morality is really "senseless conceit."[160]

Kant admitted that the life of Christ may be "nothing but miracles," but warned that in the use of these accounts "we do not make it a tenet of religion that the knowing, believing, and professing of them are themselves means whereby we can render ourselves well-pleasing to God."[161] By this he implies that it is not at all essential to the Christian faith to believe in miracles.

The very nature of a miracle is unknown to us. "We cannot know anything at all about supernatural aid," Kant wrote.[162] One thing of which we can be sure is this: if an alleged miracle "flatly contradicts morality, it cannot, despite all appearances, be of God (for example, were a father ordered to kill his son who is, so far as he knows, perfectly innocent)."[163] This would mean that Kant would use the moral law to eliminate the Abraham-Isaac story in the Old Testament (Genesis 22).

**Possible,
But Not
Rational**

Kant carried this moral argument against miracles even further. He insisted that moral reason demands that we adopt the conclusion that miracles never happen. In a revealing passage, Kant argued as follows:

> Those whose judgment in these matters is so inclined that they suppose themselves to be helpless without miracles, believe that they soften the blow which reason suffers from them by holding that they happen but *seldom*. [But we can ask] *How seldom*? Once in a hundred years? . . . Here we can determine nothing on the basis of knowledge of the object . . . but only on the basis of the maxims which are necessary to the use of our reason. Thus, miracles must be admitted as [occurring] *daily* (though indeed hidden under the guise of natural events) or else *never*. . . . Since the former alternative [that they occur daily] is not at all compatible with reason, nothing remains but to adopt the later maxim—for this principle remains ever a mere maxim for making judgments, not a theoretical assertion. [For example, with regard to the] admirable conservation of the species in the plant and animal kingdoms, . . . no one, indeed, can claim to *comprehend* whether or not the direct influence of the Creator is required on each occasion. [Kant insists] they are *for us*, . . . nothing but natural effects and *ought* never to be adjudged otherwise. . . . To venture beyond these limits is rashness and immodesty. . . .[164]

In brief, one who lives by moral reason "does not incorporate belief in miracles into his maxims (either of theoretical or practical reason), though, indeed, he does not impugn their possibility or reality."[165] So, miracles may be possible, but it is never rational to believe in them.

In view of Kant's moral form of naturalism, it is not surprising to see him reject the account of the resurrection of Christ. He wrote, "The more secret records, added as a sequel, of his *resurrection* and *ascension* . . . cannot be used in the interest of religion within the limits of reason alone without doing violence to their historical valuation. . . ."[166]

103

Are Miracles
Essential?

Summarizing
Kant's
Argument

3. *A summary of Kant's moral argument against miracles*. It is difficult to follow Kant's argument, because he implies but does not elaborate a crucial premise. But in view of what he taught elsewhere, the argument can be completed like this:

1. We cannot know the real world (the world *in itself*) by theoretical reason.[167]
2. Everything in our experience (the world *to us*) must be determined by practical reason.[168]
3. Practical reason operates according to universal laws.
4. Miracles must occur either (1) daily, (2) seldom, or (3) never.
5. But what occurs daily is not a miracle; it occurs according to natural laws.
6. And what occurs seldom is not determined by any law.
7. But everything must be determined by practical reason that operates on universal laws (2. and 3.)
8. Therefore, it is rationally necessary to conclude that miracles *never* occur.

In support of the crucial third premise, Kant wrote, "In the affairs of life, therefore, it is impossible for us to count on miracles or to take them into consideration at all in our use of reason (and reason must be used in every incident of life)."[169] In short, miracles are theoretically possible but practically impossible. That is to say, we must *live as if* they never occur. If we live otherwise, then we overthrow the whole dictates of practical reason and the moral law, which is the essence of true religion. Therefore, admitting miracles occur and living in their light is not only unnecessary to religion, it is actually harmful to it. So, even if there is a supernatural, we must live (and think) like naturalists!

II. EVALUATION OF THESE ARGUMENTS AGAINST MIRACLES

There are many things that can be said about Hobbes' and Kant's arguments. First, a few comments about Hobbes' thoughts on miracles should be considered.

A. *Comments on Hobbes' View*

**Do Miracles
Confirm
Truth?**

Hobbes' statements on miracles do not demand refutation (since he offers no real argument but rather makes assertions). First of all, it is certainly true that one ought not accept contradictions as true or mere "opinions about ghosts." Second, as Hobbes points out, mere ignorance of a natural cause does not give one the right to conclude that there was a supernatural cause. Finally, it is sometimes true that faith in the sensational fades when things return to the ordinary. Certainly the purpose of miracles ought not be to engender a dependence on the miraculous.

In the Bible, however, the purpose of miracles was to encourage dependence on God. The apostle John wrote, "Many other signs [miracles] therefore Jesus also performed . . . but these have been written *that you may believe* that Jesus is the Christ, the Son of God" (emphasis mine).[170] The writer of Hebrews speaks of miracles as *confirming* the truth God speaks through His mouthpieces: "It was confirmed to us by those who heard, God also bearing witness with them, both by signs and wonders and by various miracles" (Heb. 2:3–4). So whatever the results may be (that will depend largely on one's response), the *purpose* of biblical miracles was to confirm one's confidence in a message as the Word of God and thus encourage dependence on God Himself.

B. *Critique of Kant's Moral Argument Against Miracles*

There are many problems with Kant's argument. We will note four of them here.

**Knowing
an Unknown
World**

1. *Kant's agnosticism.* The first criticism is that agnosticism is implied in the first two premises. Kant made a radical disjunction between what he felt was the unknowable world (the *noumena*) and the world of our experience (the *phenomena*). However, phi-

losophers have often noted two things about this disjunction. First, Kant was often inconsistent with this separation, since he sometimes wandered over into the noumenal world to make statements about it, but he could do this consistently only if it is knowable. Second, one cannot consistently separate the two realms without some knowledge of *both*. The line cannot be drawn, unless one can see beyond it at least a little. In short, to say "I know that reality is unknowable" is to make a statement about reality that one claims to *know* is true. Complete agnosticism is self-defeating.

2. *Kant's rigid naturalism*. Not unlike other naturalists, Kant begs the question by laying down a uniformitarian rule. In Spinoza's case, the rule is *rational*; in Hume's case, it is *empirical*; in Flew's case, it is *methodological*, and in Kant's case, it is *moral*. But, in each case, there is some interpretive framework by which the naturalist demands a uniformitarian understanding of the world. In Kant's case, he demands regulating all of life by the universal moral law (practical reason). And since he allows no exceptions to a law, there are no exceptions to the rule that says, "Live as if there are no miracles."

But this begs the question. Why should one assume there are no exceptions or exemptions to any laws? Many of Kant's modern critics have rightly noted that this same rigid understanding of law gave him a very inflexible ethic that admitted of no exemptions to any moral commands. This rigid understanding also leads to an unrealism in conflict situations. Indeed, it is impossible to adjudicate conflicts of two or more moral laws, if both are taken to be universal without any exemptions whatsoever.[171]

3. *Kant's misunderstanding of natural law*. Kant believed, as did others of his day, that Newton's law of gravitation was *universally* true, with no exceptions. This "Newtonian" view of law as *universal* and absolutely determinable is no longer held by modern scientists. Natural law is now thought of as *general* and *statistical*, but not necessarily universal. With this view, the problem of admitting unrepeatable exceptions (which miracles would be) is resolved. But

if Kant is wrong in his view of scientific law—insisting that *every* event be subsumed under some natural law, then his moral objection to miracles fails.

4. *Kant's unhistorical attempt to desupernaturalize the Gospels*. Kant's approach to the Gospels was not historical but *moral*. Rather than looking at the historical evidence for an event (like the Resurrection), Kant summarily dismissed it as inauthentic because it was morally unessential. He admitted that this moral hermeneutic would often be "forced," but he insisted that it must be accepted rather than the "literal" understanding. Why? Not because the historical facts support it, but simply because his understanding of the moral law demanded it. In short, historical truth is determined a priori (by moral law), not a posteriori from the facts. One determines history by morality; what *is* (or was) through what *ought* to be.

5. *Why should one live by what is false?* If Kant's argument is correct, then we should live *as if* miracles do not occur—even if some have occurred! This leads to the astounding conclusion that we should order our life by a form of (practical) reason even if it is contrary to fact. Surely Freud would have called this an illusion. At any rate, if a miracle actually happened, Kant's argument would insist we live according to "reason" that says miracles do not happen. But this amounts to saying we should "reason" that what is true is false!

SUMMARY AND CONCLUSION

The attempt to show that miracles are not essential to Christianity on religious or moral grounds fails. Hobbes commends (probably with tongue in cheek) blind religious faith in the supernatural, even when it contradicts reason. Along with this fideism, he satirically reminds the reader that miracles do not really help faith anyway. This, however, is not necessarily true, at least not if the purpose of miracles is to encourage and confirm one's faith *in God* and not just to engender reliance in the sensational.

Kant's attack on miracles is more fundamental. He

sees them not only as unessential but fundamentally unnecessary to the essence of true religion: living in accordance with the universal dictates of practical reason. However, besides Kant's unjustified agnosticism, he begs the question both by assuming a moral uniformitarianism and by misunderstanding the nature of scientific "law" as universally applicable, rather than as a statistical generalization. In fact, in order for Kant to avoid the miraculous, he had to engage in some admittedly "forced" attempts to interpret the basic documents of Christianity by eliminating the Resurrection accounts without any historical reason for doing so.

Whether miracles be true or false, for better or for worse, historic Christianity claims them to be an essential part of its belief. Christianity without miracles is Christianity without Christ. So it makes a significant difference to the truth of Christianity (and its survival) as to whether or not miracles are essential to its belief. And whatever else may be said for Kant's attempt to show that miracles are not essential to religion in general, it certainly does *not* apply to Christianity in particular.

chapter nine

Are Miracles Definable?

Biblical theism is viewed as the context for the definition of a miracle. Characteristics of the theistic world view and of a legitimate miracle are reviewed.

In the previous chapters we have examined the most significant arguments against miracles from the seventeenth century to the present. In varying ways each naturalist pressed his case unsuccessfully. None succeeded in eliminating the possibility of miracles.

One thing that did emerge, however, was the need to identify a miracle before one could be known to have occurred (see chapter 5). That is, granted that miracles are identifiable in terms of some supernatural source (God), one must have some specific distinguishing characteristics of miracles in mind before he can point to a given event as one that possesses these characteristics. The question of the definition of miracles, however, is still preliminary to the actual identification of a miracle. (Whether such an identification can be made by us today will be the 109 subject of chapter 11.) We turn now to a discussion and definition of the miracles described in the Bible.

I. A Biblical Description of Miracles

There are three basic words used to describe miracles in the Bible: *sign, wonder,* and *power*. A description of the usage of each will help in understanding what is meant by a miracle.

A. *Old Testament Usage of the Words* Sign, Wonder, *and* Power

Each of the words for miracles carries with it a connotation of its own. When the meanings of all three are combined, we gain a complete picture of biblical miracles.

1. *Old Testament usage of the word* sign. Although the Hebrew word for "sign" (*oth*) is sometimes used of natural things, such as stars (Gen. 1:14) or the Sabbath (Exod. 31:13), it is most often used in a supernatural significance, namely, as something appointed by God with special assigned meaning.

The first usage of the word *sign* is in a divine prediction given to Moses that Israel would be delivered from Egypt and serve God at Horeb: God said, "Certainly I will be with you, and this shall be the sign to you that it is I who have sent you" (Exod. 3:12). When Moses asked God, "What if they will not believe me, or listen to what I say?" the Lord gave Moses two "signs": Moses' rod turned into a serpent (Exod. 4:3), and his hand turned leprous (Exod. 4:6).

These were given "that they may believe that the Lord, the God of their fathers . . . has appeared to you" (Exod. 4:5). God said, "It shall come about that if they will not believe you or heed the witness of the first sign, they may believe the witness of the last sign" (Exod. 4:8). We read that when Moses "performed the signs in the sight of the people the people believed; and . . . they bowed low and worshiped" (Exod. 4:30–31). In fact, God said, "I will harden [strengthen] Pharaoh's heart that I may multiply My signs and My wonders in the land of Egypt. . . . And the Egyptians shall know that I am the Lord, when I stretch out My hand on Egypt and bring out the sons of Israel from their midst" (Exod. 7:3, 5; cf. 11:9).

Again and again it is repeated that the purpose of these signs is twofold: "By this you shall know that I am the Lord" (Exod. 7:17)[172] and that these are "My people" (Exod. 3:10).[173] The more the Lord multiplied the signs, the harder Pharaoh's heart became (Exod. 7:3, 5; cf. 11:9). But even through this stubborn unbelief God received "glory" (Num. 14:22).

Throughout the rest of the Old Testament there are repeated references to the miraculous "signs" God performed in delivering His people from Egypt. God complained to Moses in the wilderness, saying, "How long will they not believe in me, despite all the signs which I have performed in their midst?" (Num. 14:11; cf. v. 22). Moses challenged Israel: "Has a god tried to go to take for himself nation from within another nation by trials, by signs and wonders . . . ?" (Deut. 4:34). Later Moses reminded the people, "The Lord showed great and distressing signs and wonders before our eyes against Egypt, Pharaoh and all his household" (Deut. 6:22). Often we read verses similar to Deuteronomy 26:8: "The Lord brought us out of Egypt with a mighty hand and an outstretched arm and with great terror and with signs and wonders."[174]

Signs as Confirmation

Many times in the biblical record "signs" were given to prophets as confirmation of their divine call. Moses' miraculous credentials have already been mentioned (Exodus 3 and 4). Gideon asked of God, "Show me a sign that it is Thou who speakest with me" (Judg. 6:17). God responded with miraculous fire that consumed the offering (v. 21). God confirmed Himself to Eli by miraculous predictions about his sons' deaths (1 Sam. 2:34). Likewise, predictive "signs" were made to confirm God's appointment of King Saul (1 Sam. 10:7, 9). Isaiah the prophet gave predictions as "signs" of his divine message (Isa. 7:14; 38:22). Although the word *sign* is not used in these cases, God's miraculous confirmation of Moses over Korah (Numbers 16) and Elijah over the false prophets of Baal (1 Kings 18) illustrate the same point. In short, miracles were used as signs to accredit a true prophet. Likewise, the lack of predictive powers (false prophecies) were indications that the prophet was not of God (Deut. 18:22).

Other events in the Old Testament are called "signs" or miracles as well. These include the plagues on Egypt (Exod. 7:3), the provisions in the wilderness (John 6:30–31), fire from the rock for Gideon (Judg. 6:17–21), victory over their enemies (1 Sam. 14:10), confirmation of the healing of Hezekiah (Isa. 38:7, 22), and judgments from the Lord (Jer. 44:29).

2. *Old Testament usage of the word* wonder. Often the words *signs* and *wonders* are used of the same event(s) in the same verse. Typical of these references is Exodus 7:3,[175] "that I may multiply My signs and My wonders in the land of Egypt," or, "The Lord brought us out of Egypt with a mighty hand and an outstretched arm and with great terror and with signs and wonders" (Deut. 26:8). At other times the Bible describes as "wonders" the same events that are elsewhere called "signs" (Exod. 4:21).[176] Of course sometimes the word is used of a natural "wonder," as of a prophet (Ezek. 24:24) or a unique thing a prophet did to get his message across (Isa. 20:3). But even here the "wonder" has a special supernatural (divine) significance.

"Power":
to Create,
Inspire,
Deliver

3. *Old Testament usage of the word* power. One Hebrew word for "power" (*koak*) is sometimes used of human power in the Old Testament (Gen. 31:6).[177] But very often it is used of divine power. Sometimes it is used of God's power to create: "It is He who made the earth by His power . . . and by His understanding He has stretched out the heavens" (Jer. 10:12).[178] In other places the "power" of God overthrows His enemies (Exod. 15:6–7), delivers His people from Egypt (Num. 14:17; cf. v. 13), rules the universe (1 Chron. 29:12), gives Israel their land (Ps. 111:6), and inspires His prophets to speak His Word

miracles is that it is often used in direct connection with events called "signs" or "wonders" or both (see Exod. 9:16).[179] Sometimes other Hebrew words for power are used in the same verse with "signs and wonders." Moses speaks of the deliverance of Israel "by signs and wonders . . . and by a mighty [*chazaq*] hand" (Deut. 4:34).[180]

B. *New Testament Usage of the Words* Signs, Wonders, *and* Power

The New Testament usage of the three basic words for miracles is directly parallel to that of the Old Testament. First, we will examine the word *sign* (*semeion*).

1. *New Testament usage of the word* sign. In the New Testament, *sign* (*semeion*) is used seventy-seven times (forty-eight in the Gospels). It is occasionally used of ordinary events, such as circumcision (Rom. 4:11), and even in reference to the baby Christ's swaddling clothes (Luke 2:12). But here again these *signs* have special divine significance. Most often the word *sign* is reserved for what we would call a miracle. Many times it is used of Jesus' miracles, such as healing (John 6:2; 9:16), turning the water to wine (John 2:11), and raising the dead (John 11:47). Likewise, the apostles did miracles of healing (Acts 4:16, 30), "signs and great miracles" (Acts 8:13), and "signs and wonders" (Acts 14:3; 15:12), for "many wonders and signs were taking place through the apostles" (Acts 2:43). Even the Jewish authorities said, "What shall we do with these men? For the fact that a noteworthy miracle has taken place through them is apparent to all who live in Jerusalem, and we cannot deny it" (Acts 4:16).

The word *sign* is also used of the most significant miracle in the New Testament, the resurrection of Jesus Christ from the grave. Jesus said to His unbelieving generation, "No sign shall be given to it but the sign of Jonah the prophet; . . . so shall the Son of Man be three days and three nights in the heart of the earth" (Matt. 12:39–40). Jesus repeated this prediction of His resurrection when He was asked for a "sign" in Matthew 16:1, 4. Not only was the resurrection a miracle, but it was a miracle that Jesus predicted from His early ministry (John 2:19), later (Matt. 12:40), and not many days before His death (Matt. 16:21; 20:19).

2. *New Testament usage of the word* wonder. The word *wonder* (*teras*) is used sixteen times in the New Testament and it almost always refers to a miracle.[181] In fact, in every usage it is used in combination with the word *sign*. It is used of the supernatural events before the second coming of Christ (Matt. 24:24),[182] of Jesus' miracles (John 4:48; Acts 2:22), of the apostles' miracles (Acts 2:43),[183] of Stephen's miracles (Acts 6:8), of Moses' miracles in Egypt (Acts 7:36), and of Paul's miracles (Acts 14:3).[184] The Greek word *teras* means a "miraculous sign, prodigy, portent, omen, wonder."[185] It carries with it the idea of that which is amazing or astonishing.[186]

**Divine
Energizing**

3. *New Testament usage of the word* power. The word *power* (*dunamis*) is used on numerous occasions in the New Testament. It is occasionally used of human power (2 Cor. 1:8) or abilities (Matt. 25:15). Sometimes it is used of supernatural evil (satanic) power (Luke 10:19), or of angels (or demons) themselves (Rom. 8:38). But like its Old Testament parallel, the New Testament term *power* is often translated "miracles." *Dunamis* is used in combination with "sign and wonder" (Heb. 2:4), of Christ's miracles (Matt. 11:20; 13:58), of the power to raise the dead (Phil. 3:10), of the virgin birth of Christ (Luke 1:35), of the special gift of miracles (1 Cor. 12:10), of the outpouring of the Holy Spirit at Pentecost (Acts 1:8), and of the "power" of the gospel to save sinful people (Rom. 1:16). The emphasis of the word *power* is on the *divine energizing* aspect of the miraculous event.

4. *The purposes of miracles in the New Testament*. There are several purposes of miracles indicated in the New Testament. "This beginning of His signs Jesus did in Cana of Galilee, and manifested His glory, and His disciples believed in Him" (John 2:11). John

wrote, "Many other signs therefore Jesus also per-   115
formed . . . but these have been written that you may   Are Miracles
believe that Jesus is the Christ." (John 20:30–31).   Definable?

Another purpose of miraculous "signs" is as a divine confirmation of a prophet of God. The religious ruler Nicodemus said of Jesus: "We know that you come from God as a teacher; for no one can do these signs you do unless God is with him" (John 3:2). Indeed, "a great multitude was following him, because they were seeing the signs which he was performing on those who were sick" (John 6:2). When some rejected Jesus, even though He had cured a blind man, others said, "How can a man who is a sinner perform such signs?" (John 9:16). The early apostles were confident in proclaiming, "Jesus the Nazarene is a man attested to you by God with miracles and wonders and signs which God performed through him in your midst, just as you yourselves know" (Acts 2:22). As his credentials to the Corinthians, the apostle Paul claimed that "the signs of a true apostle were performed among you" (2 Cor. 12:12). He and Barnabas recounted to the apostles "what signs and wonders God had done through them among the Gentiles" (Acts 15:12).

Perhaps the most definitive passage on miracles in the New Testament is Hebrews 2:3–4: "How shall we escape if we neglect so great a salvation? After it was at the first spoken through the Lord, it was *confirmed* to us by those [apostles] who heard, God also bearing witness with them, both by signs and wonders and by various miracles" In short, miracles are God's way of accrediting His spokesmen. There is a miracle to confirm the message as true, a sign to substantiate the sermon, an act of God to verify the Word of God.

II. A THEOLOGICAL DEFINITION OF A MIRACLE

Now that we have the essential biblical data in front of us, we are in a position to define what is meant by biblical miracle.

A. *The Nature of a Miracle*

The biblical concept of "miracle" stands in contrast to "nature." Nature is the usual, regular pattern of God's activity. As such, it can be predicted and, in this sense, "controlled" by people for their own use and benefit. Indeed nature is the domain over which God gave man dominion (Gen. 1:28). A "miracle" by contrast is unusual, unpredictable, and uncontrollable (by man). Each of the three words for supernatural events (*sign, wonder, power*) delineates an aspect of a miracle.

1. "Power" (of God) denotes its *source*— efficient cause.
2. "Wonder" conveys its *nature*—formal cause.
3. "Sign" speaks of its *purpose*—final cause.

From the human vantage point the *nature* of a miracle, then, is an unusual event ("wonder") that conveys and confirms an unusual (divine) message ("sign") by means of unusual power ("power"). From God's perspective a miracle is an *act* of God ("power") to attract the attention of the *people* of God ("wonder") to the *Word* of God ("sign").

B. *The Purpose of Miracles*

The *purpose(s)* of a miracle:

1. to glorify the nature of God (John 2:11; 11:40),
2. to accredit certain persons as the spokesmen for God (Heb. 2:3–4), and
3. to provide evidence for belief in God (John 6:2, 14; 20:30–31).

Of course, not all believe, even when they witness a miracle. But in this event, says the New Testament, the miracle is a witness against them. John grieved: "But though He [Jesus] had performed so many signs before them yet they were not believing in Him" (John 12:37). Jesus Himself said of some, "Neither will they be persuaded if someone rises from the dead'' (Luke 16:31). So in this sense the *result* (not purpose) of disbelieving in miracles is condemnation of the unbeliever (cf. John 12:31, 37).

C. *Summary of the Dimensions of Miracles*

According to the Bible, then, a miracle has several dimensions. First of all, there is the *unusual* character of a miracle. It is an unusual, out-of-the-ordinary event in contrast to the regular, normal pattern of events in the natural world. It is a ''wonder'' that attracts attention by its uniqueness. A burning bush, fire from heaven, and walking on water are not normal occurrences. Hence, they will by their unusual character draw the interest of observers.

Second, there is a *theological* dimension. A miracle is an act of God. Hence, it presupposes that there is a God who can act. The view that there is a God beyond the universe who created it, controls it, and can interfere in it is called theism. Miracles, then, imply a theistic view of the universe.

Third, miracles have a *moral* dimension. They bring glory to God. That is, they manifest the moral character of God. Miracles are visible acts that reflect the invisible nature of God. Technically, there are no evil miracles, then, because God is good. All miracles by nature aim to produce and/or promote good.*

Fourth, miracles have a *doctrinal* dimension. Miracles in the Bible are often connected with ''truth claims.'' They are ways to tell a true prophet from a false prophet (Deut. 18:22). They confirm the truth of God through the servant of God (Heb. 2:3–4). A miracle is the sign that conveys and confirms the sermon. Message and miracle go hand-in-hand.

Fifth, biblical miracles have a *teleological* dimension. They are never performed to entertain (see Luke 23:8). Miracles have distinctive purposes. Their *godward* purpose is to glorify the Creator. The *manward* purpose is to provide evidence for people to believe by accrediting the message of God through the

---

*Thus ''satanic signs'' (discussed later) are not really miracles in this sense (i.e., acts of God), even though they are supernatural, that is, caused by supernatural (but finite and evil) beings.

prophet of God. These five facets of a miracle may be said to form a theistic context for identifying a miracle.

III. THEISTIC CONTEXT FOR BIBLICAL MIRACLES

**The Need
for a
Frame of
Reference**

One essential feature of biblical miracles is their theistic context. This means that a person must be operating within a theistic world view in order to identify a miracle. To illustrate, let us consider a few incidents in the life of Moses.

Initially, when Moses came upon the burning bush (Exod. 3:1–6), he began to investigate it because of its unusual nature. The accompanying word from God, however, transformed the situation. Moses was not just in the presence of an unusual event but of a miracle. Because Moses operated within a theistic framework, he had sufficient basis to judge the event a miracle.

However, if Moses had gone back to camp and reported to Jethro, his father-in-law, what had happened—how God had spoken to him out of a burning bush—Jethro would have been entirely right to doubt the story. Thus far, the revelation and the miracle had a context that included only Moses.* If Antony Flew had walked up and argued with Jethro that the story of the burning bush was unidentified, Jethro would have been right to agree. Although Moses *knew* he was neither lying to nor deceiving Jethro, there was no way for Jethro to know that for certain (even if he was inclined to trust Moses' previously established good character and good sense). The theistic context was sufficient for Moses to believe that a miracle had taken place, but it was not sufficient for anyone else to believe it. Thus, the theistic circle of applicability included only Moses.

Later, when Moses went to Pharaoh and said, "Thus says the Lord, the God of Israel, 'Let My people go'" (Exod. 5:1), there was a wider circle of applicability. The people themselves saw unusual events happening and were able to *identify* them as

---

*This was prior to the time that Moses was publicly authenticated as a spokesman for God.

miracles. If Flew had offered them his argument that miracles were not identified, they would have had a basis to object to his argument, for they had a theistic frame of reference from which to judge. They personally had seen that aesthetic fit between prophetic word and deed, between revelation and "miracle." The Israelites knew of God's promise to deliver them from Egypt in four hundred years (Gen. 15:13–14) and they knew that, if the promised time element indicated literal years, then the time was at hand. But they did not know how God would deliver them. No doubt, some questioned whether God would deliver them at all. But it was God's promise and it was not dependent on their faith. So when Moses returned to Egypt and announced that God had told him to come back in order to lead Israel out of bondage, the Israelites had a right to question his claim. But when Moses performed the "signs" that God directed him to do, the people were inclined to believe him because of the evidence.

Then when Moses went before Pharaoh to perform the signs for him, not only were Pharaoh, the court, and the children of Israel included in the circle of applicability, but also the whole of Egypt (since, through the plagues, Moses' God was proved to be supreme, even over the gods of Egypt). In this way, the theistic context was sufficient for these unusual events to be identified as miracles. So, in this context, anyone in Israel or Egypt would have been right to reject Flew's charge that miracles were *unidentified*. But there would have been a legitimate basis for the Flews of far-away countries to doubt the miracles, because *they* were not in the circle of applicability. In short, there must be a theistic context if a miracle is to be distinguished from an unusual natural event.

IV. DISTINCTION OF MIRACLES FROM OTHER UNUSUAL EVENTS

Miracles, like anything else, can be counterfeited. And, as with good counterfeit money, the authentic is sometimes difficult to separate from the phony. In some cases only close examination of all the essential

**The
Authentic
and the
Phony**

features by a trained observer will distinguish the difference. However, in most cases the earmarks of a miracle are very clear.

A. *Miracles Differ From Anomalies*

The only similarity between a miracle and an anomaly is the unusual character of both—being odd, they both arouse interest. Beyond this there is no real similarity. Hence, simply because an event is unusual—no matter how unusual—the believer has no right to claim it is miraculous. Unless there are some theological, moral, and doctrinal purposes evident, one has no right to claim an event is a miracle. That is, there must be a theistic context for a miracle, for without signs of intelligent intervention no unusual event can be claimed to be a miracle. Odd things happen and without these divine "earmarks" they are simply that—odd. Without the other divine characteristics, the anomaly is presumed to be a natural event with a knowable cause. As scientific research proceeds, perhaps the cause will be found. On the other hand, unless the anomaly can be repeated, predicted, or brought under some natural control, there is no reason to revise any scientific law. It is simply an exception with no *known* natural explanation. In this sense, anomalies and miracles are alike. They differ in that a miracle in its theistic context gives evidence of intelligent (divine) intervention to produce the unusual event.

B. *Miracles Differ From Magic*

Here we speak not of black magic or occult activity, but simply of illusions, sleight-of-hand, or trickery. The only thing magic has in common with miracles is that both are unusual. To be sure, magic is a kind of "wonder" (Exodus 7–8). It is amazing to those who do not know the trick. But it has none of the other characteristics of a miracle. In fact, unlike an anomaly, there are known explanations for the magical wonders—known to magicians. Unlike miracles, magic as such is amoral. It does not bring glory to God (it really brings honor to the magician), and there are usually no divine truth claims connected with it. If there were supernatural claims connected with magical tricks, they could be exposed by another person who knows the tricks or by scientific tests for the hidden wires, mirrors, etc., that create the illusion.

C. *Miracles Differ From Demonic Activity*

The same biblical words used of divine miracles are used of demonic acts. Jesus warned, "False Christs and false prophets will arise and will show great signs and wonders, so as to mislead, if possible, even the elect" (Matt. 24:24). Paul warns of the anti-Christ "whose coming is in accord with the activity of Satan, with all power and signs and false wonders, and with all the deception of wickedness" (2 Thess. 2:9–10). John speaks of the "beast" to come who "performs great signs, so that he even makes fire come down out of heaven to the earth in the presence of men" (Rev. 13:13). Later, John speaks of the "spirits of demons, performing signs" (Rev. 16:14) and of the "false prophet who performed the signs . . . by which he deceived those who had received the mark of the beast and those who worshiped his image" (Rev. 19:20).

While some believers in biblical miracles have questioned whether these satanic signs should be called "miracles," there seems to be no reason to deny that they are supernatural. If a miracle by definition is an act of God that brings glory to God and good to the world, etc., then of course a demonic act is not a miracle. On the other hand, it seems evident that if one is going to believe in acts of God on the basis of the biblical record, then on this same basis he ought to believe that there are evil spirit beings who can perform highly unusual acts that the Bible calls "signs" and "wonders."[187]

If, then, the Bible claims there are at least two supernatural sources for unusual "signs" in the world, how does one tell them apart? The answer involves several "tests" (1 John 4:1) that the believer is urged to apply, all of which amount to saying that satanic "signs" have satanic (evil) characteristics and divine miracles have godlike (good) characteristics. Numerous evil indicators are mentioned in the Bible, such as idolatry (1 Cor. 10:20), immorality (Eph. 2:2), divination (Deut. 18:10), false prophecies (Deut. 18:22), occult activity (Deut. 18:14), worshiping other gods (Deut. 13:1–2), deceptive activity (2 Thess. 2:9), contacting the dead (Deut. 18:11–12), messages contrary to those revealed through true prophets (Gal. 1:8), and prophecies that do not center on Jesus Christ (Rev. 19:10).[188] And, as with any other counterfeit and deception, one must know the characteristics of good and of evil and then look carefully to see which are connected with the unusual event.

Whenever there was any serious question in the Bible as to which events were of God, a contest followed in which good triumphed over evil by an even greater miracle than the magic or satanic signs. In the contest between Moses and the Egyptian magicians, they could not reduplicate the sign of turning dust into life and gave up, crying, "This is the finger of God" (Exod. 8:18–19). In the dispute between Moses and Korah the earth opened up and swallowed Korah and company and the dispute ended abruptly (Numbers 16). Likewise, Elijah triumphed over the false prophets of Baal on Mount Carmel when fire came from heaven and consumed the water-soaked sacrifices (1 Kings 18). In the New Testament, Jesus and the apostles triumphed over evil spirits and even exorcised them (Acts 16). When necessary, the supreme God proves Himself supreme.

SUMMARY AND CONCLUSION

Summary of the Definability of Miracles

Before a miracle can be known to have occurred, it must be defined. We must know what we are looking for before we can know that we have found it. First, miracles stand in contrast to "nature," which is God's regular and predictable way of working in the world. Miracles are an unusual and unpredictable way in which God sometimes intervenes in the events of the world.

A survey of the Bible shows that a miracle is an effect that may look no different from any other unusual effect, but the characteristic feature is that it has a supernatural cause. It is performed with divine power, according to the divine mind, for a divine purpose, in order to authenticate a divine message or, perhaps, just to demonstrate God's compassion.

The biblical description of miracles uses three main words: *power, wonder,* and *sign.* Respectively, these words designate the source (in God), the nature (unusual), and the purpose of a miracle.

The miraculous event would be looked on as unusual because it does not fit some regular pattern of nature. From the scientific, observational viewpoint, it might appear to be simply an anomaly of nature, i.e., a natural event that has not yet been shown to fit a lawful pattern. But, in the case of a miracle, there would be a context of theistic claims to give it intelligibility. Without that context, which characterized Bible miracles, the alleged miracle could never have been known. It would have remained forever an "anomaly" of nature.

Spelled out in theological terms, a miracle usually manifests five characteristics: the unusual, the theological, the moral, the doctrinal, and the teleological. Miracles can be distinguished from anomalies and magic, since the latter two share only one of these characteristics—the unusual.

While satanic signs are not amoral, they do differ from miracles in their discernibly evil characteristics. In short, biblical miracles are acts of God to confirm the Word of God through a prophet of God to the people of God.

Finally, we can conclude that miracles are possible only within a theistic universe. If God exists, then miracles are possible. Further, if God exists, then miracles are identifiable in terms of some Godlike characteristics (theological, moral, etc.).

With such a definition of miracles, one can proceed to examine any possible miracle. There are certainly many events that have been claimed to be miraculous. But are there any events that can be *known* to be miraculous? This will be the subject of chapter 11.

chapter ten

Are Miracles Antinatural?

Biblical miracles are compared and contrasted with al-
leged miracles from other historical contexts. The modern
objection that miracles are antinatural is evaluated in the
light of a contemporary conception of nature.

Innumerable implausible events that many people
believed were miracles are alleged to have occurred.
But to the modern mind these events appear to be
incredible. One of the underlying and residual obsta-
cles regarding miracles, for modern thinkers, is that
they seem so unnatural as to be antinatural. That is,
some miracles appear to be not only extraordinary but
bizarre. They seem so odd as to be unbelievable.
When one thinks of some of the weird and outlandish
stories that have been believed by both pagans and
Christians as miraculous events, this is an under-
standable (even justifiable) reaction.

I. The Oddity of Some Miracle Stories

A. *Early Miracle Stories About Christ*

During the second and third centuries there were numerous books written by various religious groups that related bizarre stories about the childhood of Christ. One such miracle story, as follows, speaks of the whole course of nature standing still at Christ's birth.

> I looked up at the vault of heaven, and saw it standing still and the birds of the heaven motionless. And I looked at the earth, and saw a dish placed there and workmen lying round it, with their hands in the dish. But those who chewed did not chew, and those who lifted up anything lifted up nothing. . . . And behold, sheep were being driven and (yet) they did not come forward, but stood still. . . . And I looked at the flow of the river, and saw the mouths of the kids over it and they did not drink. And then all at once everything went on its course (again).[189]

The child Jesus, likewise, is said to have performed some highly unnatural events. As a five-year-old lad playing in the brook,

> He made soft clay and fashioned from it twelve sparrows. . . . Jesus clapped his hands and cried to the sparrows: "Off with you!" And the sparrows took flight and went away chirping. [The story continues,] But the son of Annas the scribe was standing there with Joseph; and he took a branch of a willow and (with it) dispersed the water which Jesus had gathered together. When Jesus saw what he had done he was enraged and said to him: "You insolent, godless dunderhead, what harm did the pools and the water do to you?" [Forthwith Jesus cursed him] and immediately that lad withered up completely.[190]

When Jesus was blamed for the death of a neighbor boy, "immediately those who had accused him became blind."[191]

On another occasion Joseph cut off a beam too short. Jesus said, "Put down the two pieces of wood and make them even from the middle to one end." Joseph obeyed, "and Jesus stood at the other end and took hold of the shorter piece of wood, and stretching it made it equal with the other."[192]

If these miracle stories are contrary to the way the world operates, some of the saints' miracles in the middle ages seem "out of this world."

B. *Some Medieval Miracle Stories*

Paul Sabatier, in his *Life of Francis of Assisi*, cites a number of odd miracle stories. "In one case a parrot being carried away by a kite uttered the invocation dear to his master, '*sancte Thoma, adjuva me*,' [Saint Thomas, save me] and was immediately rescued." In another case, "A merchant of Groningen, having purloined an arm of St. John the Baptist, grew rich as if by enchantment, so long as he kept it concealed in his house, but was reduced to beggary so soon as . . . the relic was taken away from him and placed in a church."[193]

More Odd Stories

Some stories of religious relic miracles are also bizarre. "Bernard of Clairvaux, for example, when in extremities, needed to be saved from without—by the intervention of Mary, who gave him her breast."[194] One writer claimed this "mysticism of the Mary-legend brought a new means of healing, in that it makes Mary give her breast to the sick." In one case "a cleric in his illness had bitten off his tongue and lips, and was suddenly healed by Mary's milk." When the healing power of the milk was observed, it was "gathered up and saved as a relic"[195]

Other reported medieval miracles include the "stigmata" or bleeding wounds of a living saint in emulation of Jesus' wounds[196] and St. Anne's wrist bone, which is called the "Great Relic" and which was venerated by thousands of people, reportedly resulting in some healings.[197] Even modern Roman Catholic scholars defend both of these kinds of "miracles" and the veneration of relics.[198]

Some medieval miracle stories are so farfetched as to be literally impossible or ridiculously doubtful. In one case, a saint allegedly placed his decapitated head in his mouth and then swam across a river! What are we to think of such stories?

II. EVALUATION OF THESE MIRACLE STORIES

One thing that strikes the intelligent reader about some of these miracles is that they are not really *super*natural; most of them are really *contra*natural. How, for example, can the whole course of nature freeze for a few moments and then resume? Surely it is impossible to put one's head in one's own mouth! And even if it were, what possible use would the God of the Bible have for such an act? The miracles of the Bible, though unusual and obviously divine in their origin, show forth clearly the character of God. They demonstrate purpose and order, something these more recent miracle stories do not. Even some of the alleged childhood miracles of Jesus do not really fit into the natural world. Indeed, these apocryphal miracles are very unlike the miracles of the Bible.

As C. S. Lewis, an Oxford literary scholar, put it, "If we open such books as Grimm's *Fairy Tales* or Ovid's *Metamorphoses* or the Italian epics we find ourselves in a world of miracles so diverse that they can hardly be classified." In them "beasts turn into men and men into beasts or trees, trees talk, ships become goddesses, and a magic ring can cause tables richly spread with food to appear in solitary places." If such things really happened, they would "show that Nature was being invaded. But they would show that she was being invaded by an alien power."[199] These fantasies, like many early and medieval Christian miracles, do not really fit into nature. Indeed, some early and medieval miracle stories bear a much stronger resemblance to fantasy stories than to the biblical records of miracles. They are in fact clearly antinatural.

III. BIBLICAL MIRACLES ARE NOT ANTINATURAL

Biblical miracles stand in strong contrast to these apocryphal miracles and fairy tales. The miracles of the New Testament are not contranatural. "The fitness of the Christian miracles," wrote Lewis, "and their difference from these mythological miracles, lies in the fact that they show invasion by a Power which is not alien." They are, in fact, "what might be expected to happen when she is invaded not simply by a god, but by the God of Nature: by a Power which is outside her jurisdiction not as a foreigner but as a sovereign."[200]

A. *The General Nature of Christian Miracles Is Not Contranatural*

Biblical miracles are not against nature; many are largely a speeding up of natural processes. "I contend," said Lewis, "that in all these [biblical] miracles alike the incarnate God does *suddenly* and *locally* something that God has done or will do in general" (emphasis mine). That is to say, "Each miracle writes for us in small letters something that God has already written, or will write, in letters almost too large to be noticed, across the whole canvas of Nature." Hence, "Not one of them is isolated or anomalous: each carries the signature of the God whom we know through conscience and from Nature. Their authenticity is attested by the *style*."[201]

The point here is simply, If God exists and is the author of our (inward) moral nature and of (external) physical nature, we already know His "style" of working (cf. Acts 17:29; Rom. 1:19–20; 2:12–14). Therefore, so-called miracles that are against this style (contranatural) are judged inauthentic, and miracles in this style can be considered authentic. For God may wish to perfect the form of things He has made, but He does not work (even by miracles) against His work.

B. *The Specific Nature of New Testament* Miracles Is Not Contranatural*

Of course, knowing God's "style" is not automatic, any more than is knowing the style of any great artist. It takes the training of one's moral and

---

*Space does not permit a treatment of Old Testament miracles, but they too fit into nature just as New Testament miracles do. Some Old Testament miracles are healings (2 Kings 5); some are resurrections (2 Kings 4) and the like (Jonah 2). Others utilize theological faculties (Heb. 5:14) to recognize the moral and theological dimensions of a miracle. Jesus performed many miracles in the Gospels. The first of these was the conversion of water into wine (John 2). Other than the unusual suddenness of the event, this should not be surprising to one who is accustomed to God's way of working in natural processes. "In a certain sense, He constantly turns water into wine, for wine, like all drinks, is but water modified. Once, and in one year only, God, now incarnate, short circuits the process: makes wine in a moment. . . . The Miracle consists in the *short cut*; but the event to which it leads is the usual one."[202]

God's Creative Power

The two cases of miraculous feeding of thousands (Matt. 14:15-21; 15:32-38) falls into this same category. "They involve the multiplication of a little bread and a little fish into much bread and much fish." Again, this is not contranatural. For "every year God makes a little corn into much corn: the seed is sown and there is an increase."[203] The same pattern is seen in multiplied fish. "Look down into every bay and almost every river. This swarming, undulating fecundity shows He is still at work 'thronging the seas with spawn innumerable.' " Thus, it is not contranatural for Jesus to multiply fish. For it was God "who at the beginning commanded all species 'to be fruitful and multiply and replenish the earth.' And now, that day, at the feeding of the thousands, incarnate God does the same; does close and small, under His human hands . . . what He has always been doing in the seas, the lakes and the little brooks."[204]

---

natural elements and animals—plagues in Egypt (Exod. 7-12) or earthquakes (Num. 16:28-34). The Red Sea was divided by the natural force of wind (Exod. 14:21), and even the manna from heaven came with the natural night dew (Exod. 16:11-15). It is evident that Jesus and the New Testament writers did not view the Old Testament events as myths (cf. 1 Tim. 4:6-7; 2 Tim. 4:4; Titus 1:10-14). Jesus affirmed the historicity of Adam and Eve (Matt. 19:4-5), Noah and the flood (Matt. 24:37-39), Jonah and the whale (Matt. 12:40), the serpent story in the wilderness (John 3:14), Elijah's miracles (Luke 4:26), and numerous other events, most of which had miraculous elements.

To some the Virgin Birth seems to be a quite contranatural way to be born. To be sure, it is unnatural,
but it is not thereby *contra*natural. Some consider it a
slur on sexual intercourse. This, however, is no more
true than feeding the five thousand is an insult to
bakers.[205] Something about the event had to be highly
unusual, otherwise it would not qualify as a miracle.
And having no male fertilization is highly unusual.
However, this does not make the virgin birth of Christ
contranatural, for two basic reasons.

First, even the Virgin Birth resulted in a natural
nine-month pregnancy and natural childbirth. Furthermore,

> if we believe that God created Nature that momentum
> [i.e., creation of life] comes from Him. The human
> father is merely an instrument, a carrier . . . simply the
> last in a long line of carriers—a line that stretches back
> far beyond his ancestors . . . back to the creation of
> matter itself. That line is in God's hand. It is the instru-
> ment by which He normally creates a man.[206]

In short, ultimately God's creative powers are necessary in every birth, to say nothing of a virgin birth.
The main difference, then, is not that one is natural
and the other antinatural. It is that one is a direct and
the other an indirect use of God's creative power.

**An
Acted
Parable**

Jesus also performed many healing miracles. This
too is not against nature. There is a sense in which the
doctor never heals anything; nature heals. More properly God heals through natural processes. Hence,
other than the unusual speed by which Jesus healed,
there is nothing essentially contrary to nature in a
physical healing. After all, Jesus did not create special radar for the blind or produce bionic legs for the
lame. He healed natural eyes and strengthened natural
legs. Even the one so-called "negative" miracle that
Jesus performed, cursing the fig tree so that it with-
ered, is not antinatural. For that is precisely what fig
trees ultimately do—wither and die. (And even this
"negative" miracle He did not perform without a
positive purpose. For this miracle is an acted parable,
a symbol of God's desire to see His people be fruit-

ful.) Of course, simply because these miracles are not contrary to nature does not ipso facto make them natural. Their unusual and "divine" dimensions qualify them as supernatural.

On occasion Jesus raised the dead. Does not the natural mortality of all men render resurrection miracles as contranatural? Here again the response is: contrary to the usual, "yes," but contrary to the natural, "no." The desire to live on after death is virtually universal to mankind. Certainly it is not an uncommon desire. Further, the reversal of death and decay is not against nature; it is in fact *for* nature's rejuvenation. As C. S. Lewis aptly puts it, "Entropy by its very character assures us that though it may be the universal rule in the Nature we know, it cannot be universal absolutely." For

> a Nature which is "running down" cannot be the whole story. A clock can't run down unless it has been wound up. . . . If a Nature which disintegrates order were the whole of reality, where would she find any order to disintegrate? Thus on any view there must have been time when processes the reverse of those we now see were going on: a time of winding up.[207]

And if it was once "natural" to generate life that is now degenerating, then it is not unnatural if it be regenerated (via resurrection). Indeed, this is what is involved in the "grand miracle"[208] of the death and resurrection of Christ.

And if resurrection is not against the natural, then the other miracles of the "new creation,"* such as Christ's transfiguration, walking on water, and otherwise dominating nature may just be foretastes or "firstfruits" (1 Cor. 15:20) of the new nature to come (Rev. 21:1–5). This domination of nature by spirit is by no means contranatural. For the "Spirit by dominating Nature confirms and improves natural activities. The brain does not become less a brain by being used for rational thought."[209]

---

*Lewis makes two broad categories of miracles: first, miracles of the "old creation" that basically accelerate nature; second, those of the "new creation" that regenerate nature or what nature will be like after Christ's return. See C. S. Lewis, *Miracles*, chapters 15 and 16.

Let us now summarize the similarities and differences between a miracle and a natural process. First of all, both have the *same source*—God. Neither nature nor miracle is self-caused. Both find their root in the supernatural. Nature is the result of the first great miracle—creation. A miracle involves a similar but smaller creative intervention of God. It is an event in the natural world that would not have happened were nature left to itself.*

Second, a miracle is *physically similar* to nature. It is similar to the natural process. Many miracles are simply a speeding up of a natural process. They are a shortcut to what nature does regularly. They are a microcosm of the macrocosm of nature. Other miracles improve nature and anticipate her regeneration (resurrection). In fact, nature itself rehearses annually and seasonally its own regeneration with autumn (death) and spring (life). So then all miracles *fit* into the natural world and natural expectations.

Third, there is a *moral similarity* between miracles and nature. Miracles—acts of God—are like God. They are in accord with the natural moral law of God (cf. Rom. 2:12–15). No miracles have evil or destructive purposes; rather their purposes are good. They are in accord with the natural law of God. So then miracles have a good purpose and goal—the ultimate deliverance of the natural world (Rom. 8:19–21).

Fourth, nature and miracles *differ in their regularity* and predictability. Nature operates in regular and predictable patterns, and it is thus under man's control (Gen. 1:28). Miracles are by nature irregular and unpredictable by man and, hence, are not under man's control. But even here the origin of the natural world is an unrepeatable singular event, as is a miracle.

In short, biblical miracles come from *beyond* nature; they *befit* nature and they *benefit* nature. Their source is *God*; their nature is *Godlike*, and their goal

Are Miracles Antinatural?

Microcosms of Nature

---

*Some supernaturalists would say that a miracle is what nature "could not" do on its own without intelligent (divine) intervention.

is *good*. Many extrabiblical "miracles" lack these characteristics and some are even contranatural.

SUMMARY AND CONCLUSION

Throughout history, both pagan and Christian, many bizarre events have been claimed as miraculous. However, many of these events do not fit into nature, and some are even contrary to nature. Hence, they do not have the required theistic context to qualify as miracles. They have neither the divine context (revelation)* nor the divine style.

This is not the case with biblical miracles. They not only fit into nature but even perfect nature. Biblical miracles are not *anti*natural; they are simply *un*natural. That is, they are not *contra*natural, but *super*natural. They are not against nature but do claim to come from beyond nature. However, they are not unlike nature, for nature bears the resemblance of its Creator (see Ps. 19:1–4). Indeed, many biblical miracles are largely a speeding up of natural processes. All fit into nature. Some anticipate the renewal and regeneration of nature but never its ultimate destruction. Just as a nature that is "running down" was once "wound up," so resurrection and new creation miracles signal the "rewinding" or regeneration of nature. In this regard, biblical miracles are far from *against* natire. They are *for* nature by coming from *beyond* it and by working to perfect what is *within* it. The same cannot be said for many of the bizarre and apocryphal events recorded outside the Bible, which have also claimed to be miraculous.

---

*The "miracles" of the apocryphal books and of religious cults are all connected with doctrines contrary to biblical teaching. Hence, they can be judged false on this ground (see chapter 9). God never vindicates falsehood by a supernatural act.

Are Miracles Actual?

The authenticity and credibility of New Testament miracles are considered in the light of David Hume's objections and of the reliability of the biblical documents.

Thus far we have discussed the possibility of miracles. The antisupernaturalist's charges have been examined and found lacking. Miracles have not been proved to be either impossible or incredible (see chapters 1 and 2). They have not been shown to be either unscientific or unidentifiable (see chapters 3, 4, and 5). Further, biblical miracles are not mythological but claim to be historical (see chapters 6 and 7). Neither can miracles be ruled out as nonessential to Christianity nor undefinable (see chapters 8 and 9). Further, miracles are unusual but they are not antinatural (see chapter 10). For, if God exists, then miracles are possible because of His control over the world, and they are definable in terms of His character manifest in the world. The root question, then, is one of theism or atheism.

135

The remaining question is this: Are miracles *actual*? That is to say, granting the context of a theistic universe that would make miracles possible and identifiable, can an event be identified as a miracle? Or, if God exists, what (if any) event(s) from His perspective can be called miraculous?

Purposeful Divine Activity

Before answering the question of whether miracles are actual, we should point out the difference between the supernaturalist and naturalist views in assessing reality. By definition, in naturalism everything that happens is natural. No criterion is needed to judge an unusual event. Because everything is natural, viewing reality is simple.

For the supernaturalist, viewing reality is not so easy. There are both natural and supernatural events. Making the distinction *requires* a criterion. The natural is regular, repeatable, and predictable; it is characterized by generalized effects from generalized causes. The supernatural is irregular, unrepeatable (usually), and unpredictable; it is characterized by specific effects that manifest intelligent, purposeful, divine activity. The appearance of an unusual or strange event presents a difficulty, so supernaturalists must be careful in their thinking. By definition, the event is strange, since it does not fit the regular pattern of *known* lawful behavior. Do supernaturalists automatically appeal to the supernatural to explain this strange event? This is the great fear of naturalists. It is their stereotype of what supernaturalists will do. Although some supernaturalists have taken this easy way out, the stereotype is not realistic.

Admittedly, some believers have made mistakes by attempting to identify as miracles some unusual events that later were scientifically understood to be natural events. Had it been noted that these unusual events lacked the proper accompanying theistic characteristics, much embarrassment could have been avoided.

The way of truth is not always easy. One must determine whether an unusual event has occurred in a theistic context before the event can be identified as a miracle.

As we have already seen, within a theistic world, the answer to the actuality of miracles is not a metaphysical one; it is an empirical one. That is, the *possibility* of miracles can be established philosophically, but the *actuality* of miracles can only be established historically.

I. HUME'S OBJECTION AGAINST WITNESSES

Since we are not primarily concerned here with miracle claims in general or even with current claims for the miraculous, but simply with the miracles of the New Testament, the question boils down to the authenticity of the New Testament documents and the credibility of the New Testament witnesses. This brings us to a confrontation with a final argument of David Hume.

A. *Hume's Argument Stated*

Hume really had two arguments against the witnesses to miracles. The first one would rule out testimony to miracles *in principle*. This argument would eliminate belief in miracles *in advance* of looking at the evidence. Since we have already shown in chapter 2 that such a priori attempts to eliminate miracles have all failed, our concern here is with Hume's a posteriori argument. That is to say, *in practice*, is there enough evidence to establish New Testament miracles?

Hume enumerates four arguments against the actuality of miracles (including those of the New Testament).

1. *A sufficient number of good witnesses is lacking*. First of all, says Hume, "there is not to be found, in all history, any miracle attested by a sufficient number of men of such unquestioned good-sense, education, and learning as to secure us against all delusion in themselves." Nor are there enough witnesses of "such undoubted integrity, as to place them beyond all suspicion of any design to deceive others." Neither are they "of such credit and reputation in the

eyes of mankind, as to have a great deal to lose in case of their being detected in any falsehood." Finally, neither have the alleged miracles been "performed in such a public manner and in so celebrated a part of the world as to render the detection unavoidable."[210]

2. *Knowledge of human nature renders miracle stories suspect*. "We may observe in human nature a principle which, if strictly examined, will be found to diminish extremely the assurance which we might, from human testimony, have in any prodigy." Just "the strong propensity of mankind to the extraordinary and marvelous . . . ought reasonably to beget suspicion against all relations of this kind." And "if the spirit of religion join itself to the love of wonder, there is an end of common sense," wrote Hume.[211] Add to this such things as "enthusiasm," "vanity," and "self-interest," and one can easily account for delusion about miracles.

3. *Miracles abound chiefly among the ignorant*. Third, says Hume, "it forms strong presumption against all supernatural and miraculous relations that they are observed chiefly to abound among ignorant and barbarous nations." And "if a civilized people has ever given admission to any of them, that people will be found to have received them from ignorant and barbarous ancestors. . . ." Further, "the advantages are so great of starting an imposture among ignorant people that . . . it has a much better chance for succeeding in remote countries than if the first scene had been laid in a city renowned for arts and knowledge."[212]

4. *Miracle claims have a self-canceling nature*. The final argument offered by Hume is that "there is no testimony for [an alleged miracle] that is not opposed by an infinite number of witnesses; so that not only the miracle destroys the credit of testimony, but the testimony destroys itself." That is, "every miracle, therefore, pretended to have been wrought in any of these religions (and all of them abound in miracles) . . . so has it the same force, though more indirectly, to overthrow every other system" and "in destroying a rival system, it likewise destroys the credit of those miracles on which that system was established."

In short, since a miracle's "direct scope is to establish the particular system to which it is attributed, so has it the same force . . . to overthrow every other system."[213] Miracles, being all of the same kind, are self-canceling as witnesses to the truth of a religious system.

Hume sums it all up in these words: "Upon the whole, then, it appears that no testimony for any kind of miracle has ever amounted to a probability, much less to a proof." Further, "even supposing it amounted to a proof, it would be opposed by another proof derived from the very nature of the fact which it would endeavour to establish."[214]

B. *An Evaluation of Hume's Criticisms*

Even though Hume's argument appears to imply that he is really open to the actual evidence for or against a miracle, it turns out that he has here again ruled out in advance the credibility claims for any miracle. This is evident for a number of reasons.

First, Hume admits that *no amount of witnesses* would convince him of a miracle. Speaking of what he admitted were highly attested Jansenist miracles of his day, Hume wrote: "And what have we to oppose to such a cloud of witnesses but the *absolute impossibility* or miraculous nature of the events which they relate?" (emphasis mine). And this, Hume adds, "surely, in the eyes of all reasonable people, will alone be regarded as a sufficient refutation."[215] So, no matter how many witnesses one provides for these "absolutely impossible" events, no "reasonable person" will believe them. If this is the case, then Hume is still approaching every miraculous event, no matter how well it is attested, with an incurably naturalistic bias. All the talk of testing the credibility of the witnesses is a poorly concealed disguise for an intractable antisupernaturalism.

Second, Hume would not allow testimony for miracles, and yet he would allow testimony of those who had seen water frozen in preference to the testimony of those who never had. But why allow testimony for one event and not for the other, unless it is simply a matter of his prejudice against miracles?

Third, Hume's last argument (above) is but a cover for his naturalism. For, on Hume's assumption (that all religions have like miracles), no matter how many thousands of good witnesses one produces, the event cannot be claimed as a miracle. In fact, Hume says each miracle will be "opposed by an *infinite number* of witnesses" (emphasis mine).[216] This means that, in actual fact, *Hume would not allow any amount of evidence to count for any miracle claim*. Here too his naturalistic bias is incorrigible. His absolute faith in naturalism is actually unfalsifiable!

However, before Hume's argument is dismissed as being of no value, it should be pointed out that it is a sound argument against all non-Christian miracle claims that are supported by like (but inferior) miracles to those performed by Christ. We may restate the argument this way.

1. All non-Christian religions are supported by like "miracles."
2. But such "miracles" have no evidential value (since they are self-canceling and based on poor testimony).
3. Therefore, no non-Christian religion is supported by miracles.

If this is so, then one can argue, in addition, that only Christianity is confirmed as true via miracles.

1. Only Christianity has unique miraculous confirmation of its truth claims based on sufficient testimony (see below).
2. What has unique miraculous confirmation of its truth claims is true (and all opposing views are false).
3. Therefore, Christianity is true (and all opposing views are false).

Three Important Premises

There are, of course, three important premises to establish in this argument: (1) that the Christian miracles have actually occurred, (2) that these miracles are unique, and (3) that the testimony is sufficient.

All of these questions are involved in the authenticity of the New Testament. We now examine the historicity of these records.

II. THE EVIDENCES FOR NEW TESTAMENT MIRACLES

There are two basic questions to answer before one can know if New Testament miracles actually occurred. The first is the reliability of the documents, and the second is the integrity of the witnesses.

A. *Are the New Testament Documents Reliable?*

It may seem a gross exaggeration, to one not familiar with the evidence, to claim that there is more documentary evidence for the reliability of the New Testament than for any other book from the ancient world. But it is true, nonetheless. The evidence for this claim is abundant.

1. *The New Testament has more manuscripts*. It is not uncommon for some of the great classics from antiquity to survive in only a handful of manuscript copies. According to the great Manchester biblical scholar F. F. Bruce, we have about nine or ten good copies of Caesar's *Gallic War*, twenty copies of Livy's *Roman History*, two copies of Tacitus's *Annals*, and eight manuscripts of Thucydides' *History*.[217] The most documented secular work from the ancient world is Homer's *Iliad*, surviving in some 643 manuscript copies. By contrast, there are now over *5,300* Greek manuscripts of the New Testament. *The New Testament is the most highly documented book from the ancient world!**

2. *The New Testament has earlier manuscripts*. One of the marks of a good manuscript is its age. Generally the older the better, since the closer to the time of original composition, the less likely it is that the text has been corrupted. Most books from the ancient world survive not only in a handful of manuscripts but in manuscripts that were written about *one thousand years* after they were originally composed. This is true of the above books. (It is rare to have, as

---

*"Book" here means anything written on papyri or manuscript material. There are, of course, many original clay tablets that have been preserved.

the *Odyssey* does, one manuscript copied only five hundred years after the original.) The New Testament, by contrast, survives in complete books from a little over a hundred and fifty years after the books were composed, and one fragment[218] survives from within about a generation of the time it was composed. *No other book from the ancient world has a smaller time gap* (between composition and earliest manuscript copies) *than does the New Testament*.

**An
Accurate
Copy**

3. *The New Testament is more accurately copied.* It is safe to say that the New Testament is the most accurately copied book from the ancient world. There is widespread misunderstanding about the so-called errors in the biblical manuscripts. Some have estimated some 200,000 of them. First of all, these are not really "errors" but only *variant* readings, the vast majority of which are strictly grammatical. Second, these readings are spread throughout more than 5,300 manuscripts, so that a variant spelling of one letter of one word in one verse in 3,000 manuscripts is counted as 3,000 "errors." Third, these 200,000 variants represent only some 10,000 places in the New Testament. Fourth, the famous textual scholars Westcott and Hort estimated that only 1/60th of these variants rise above "trivialities." This would leave a text 98.33 percent pure.[219] The great scholar A. T. Robertson said that the real concern is only with a "thousandth part of the entire text." This would make the New Testament 99.9 percent free of significant variants. The noted historian Philip Schaff calculated that, of the 150,000 variants known in his day, only 400 affected the meaning of the passage, only 50 were of real significance, and *not even one* affected "an article of faith or a precept of duty which is not abundantly sustained by other and undoubted passages, or by the whole tenor of Scripture teaching."[220]

To illustrate how a copyist's error does not affect either substantial meaning or message, note the following telegram:

or

"YO# HAVE WON A MILLION DOLLARS."

If we received a telegram with hundreds of lines, each one of which had a similar mistake, we still would say that the message is beyond all reasonable doubt. Now it is noteworthy that the New Testament manuscripts have a smaller percentage of significant copyist errors than this telegram. Further, with 5,300 manuscripts (compared to a few lines), the real message of the New Testament is no more affected than is the message of the telegram.

By comparison with the New Testament, most other books from the ancient world are not nearly so well authenticated. The well-known New Testament scholar Bruce Metzger estimated that the *Mahabharata* of Hinduism is copied with only about 90 percent accuracy and Homer's *Iliad* with about 95 percent. By comparison, he estimated the New Testament is about 99.5 percent accurate.[221] So, by even conservative standards, the New Testament survives in the reconstructed text with about 99 percent accuracy and 100 percent of the message coming through.

In summation of the evidence, the noted textual scholar Sir Frederic Kenyon may be quoted.

> The number of manuscripts of the New Testament, of early translations from it, and of quotations from it in the oldest writers of the Church, is so large that it is practically certain that the true reading of every doubtful passage is preserved in some one or other of these ancient authorities. This can be said of no other ancient book in the world.[222]

B. *Are the Witnesses Reliable?*

Tracing the manuscripts back to the first century does not prove, of course, that those who wrote them were either honest or accurate. In order to establish the authenticity of what the manuscripts say, one must examine the evidence relating to the witnesses.

Eyewitness Authors

To begin with, the New Testament was composed by eyewitnesses. Most (if not all) of the New Testament claims to be written by eyewitnesses and contemporaries of the events of Jesus' ministry (ca. A.D. 29–33). Matthew is written by an observer who gives long and direct quotes from Jesus (e.g., 5–7; 13; 23; 24–25). He was accustomed to taking records as a tax collector (Matt. 9:9). Mark was a disciple of Peter (1 Peter 5:13) and an eyewitness of Christ (2 Peter 1:16). Luke was an educated contemporary of Christ who said that "just as those who from the beginning were eyewitnesses and servants of the word" (viz., the apostles), so too "it seemed fitting for me as well, having investigated everything carefully from the beginning, to write it out for you in consecutive order . . ." (Luke 1:1–3). John the apostle was a direct eyewitness (John 21:24; cf. 1 John 1:1), as was Peter (2 Peter 1:16). Paul was a contemporary of Christ and a witness of His resurrection (1 Cor. 15:8). Paul lists dozens of others who saw the resurrected Christ, together with a group of over five hundred, most of whom were still alive when he wrote (1 Cor. 15:6).

The evidence that these claims should be taken at face value is weighty. First, there is the general rule of historical research expressed by Immanuel Kant. This rule says in effect that historical reports are "innocent until proven guilty." That is, what purports to be authentic should be accepted as authentic, until it is shown to be inauthentic. As Kant pointed out, this is indeed the rule used in the normal discourses of life. Were the opposite used, there would be a total breakdown of communication.

Courtroom-Worthy Evidence

Second, there is what is known in law as the "ancient document rule." According to this rule, "a writing is sufficiently authenticated as an ancient document if the party who offers it satisfies the judge that the writing is thirty years old, that it is unsuspicious in appearance, and further proves that the writing is produced from a place of custody natural for such a document." According to the legal authority McCormick, "Any combination of circumstances sufficient to support a finding of genuineness will be appropriate authentication."[223] Now, using the rule, the New Testament should be considered authentic. It is an ancient document whose transmission can be traced and whose custodianship has been proper. In fact, many great legal minds have been convinced of the truth of Christianity on the basis of the rules of evidence used to try life-and-death cases in the courtroom. In point of fact Simon Greenleaf, a professor of law who wrote the book on legal evidence, was converted to Christianity in just this way.[224]

Third, there is the early dating of the New Testament manuscripts. The most knowledgeable scholars date the New Testament books within the lifetime of the eyewitnesses and alleged authors. Noted archaeologist Nelson Glueck wrote, "We can already say emphatically that there is no longer any solid basis for dating any book of the New Testament after about A.D. 80. . . ."[225] The renowned paleographer William F. Albright declared that "every book of the New Testament was written by a baptized Jew between the forties and the eighties of the first century A.D. (very probably between about A.D. 50 and 75)."[226] Recently, even the radical "death-of-God" theologian Bishop John Robinson of *Honest to God*[227] fame has become honest with the facts and declared that the New Testament was written between A.D. 40 and 65.[228] This would mean that the basic New Testament documents were written by contemporaries *only seven years or so after the events* and were circulated among other eyewitnesses and/or contemporaries of the events.

Fourth, the science of archaeology has confirmed the historical accuracy of the Gospel records. This can be dramatically illustrated through the writings of Sir William Ramsay, whose conversion from a skeptical view of the New Testament was supported by a lifetime of research in the Near Eastern world. Ramsay speaks for himself.

"Narrative Showed Marvelous Truth"

> I began with a mind unfavorable to it [Acts], for the ingenuity and apparent completeness of the Tübingen theory had at one time quite convinced me. It did not lie

then in my line of life to investigate the subject minutely; but more recently I found myself often brought in contact with the book of *Acts* as an authority for the topography, antiquities, and society of Asia Minor. It was gradually borne in upon me that in various details the narrative showed marvellous truth.[229]

Ramsay discovered that Luke was a first-rate historian. In Luke's references to thirty-two countries, fifty-four cities, and nine islands, there are *no errors*! Then Luke's narration of the life and miracles of Christ must likewise be accepted as authentic. And since Luke's narration of Christ's life and miracles is in accord with that of the other Gospels, we have here an archaeological confirmation of the Gospels that record the miracles and resurrection of Christ.

Not Intrinsically Improbable

Of course, some would argue that the miraculous events recorded in the New Testament are intrinsically improbable, so that no amount of testimony would lead one to believe them. No parents would believe a child who said there was a green monster in the bedroom, whereas they would examine the room if the child claimed there was a hornet there. The theists' response to this, however, is to point out that one can only postulate intrinsic improbability against miracles if one has good reason in advance to believe there is no God. If, however, there is no good reason to eliminate God, but on the contrary there is good reason to believe in Him (see chapter 5), then one should not rule out miracles in advance as intrinsically improbable.

In summary, from a strictly *historical* point of view, one could not have better evidence for the authenticity of events than we possess for the central events in the life of Christ.

C. *Cross-examining the Witnesses for the Resurrection*

Christianity's Cornerstone Miracle

The great miracle of Christianity is the death and resurrection of Christ. If these events are true, all other New Testament miracles are easily believable. Indeed, in many respects the Resurrection is the cornerstone miracle of Christianity. The apostle Paul was willing to concede that "if Christ has not been raised, then our preaching is vain, your faith also is vain" (1 Cor. 15:14). In fact, Jesus used His resurrection as a proof of His deity (Matt. 12:40; John 2:19; 20:28). Christianity stands or falls on this event. If it is true, then it substantiates what Jesus claimed to be.* If it is false, then not only is Christianity false but the case for the credibility of biblical miracles is seriously shaken. What then is the evidence for the miraculous resurrection of Christ? How sufficient are the witnesses?

David Hume outlined the basic criteria that he believed necessary for testing the credibility of witnesses. In his own words:

> We entertain suspicion concerning any matter of fact when (1) the witnesses contradict each other, (2) when they are but few or (3) of a doubtful character, (4) when they have an interest in what they affirm, (5) when they deliver their testimony with hesitation, or with too violent asseverations.[230]

Basically, these can be translated into these questions: (1) Do the witnesses contradict each other? (2) Are there a sufficient number of witnesses? (3) Were the witnesses of good character? (4) Was their testimony prejudicial? (5) Were there any signs of perjury? (lying)? Let us apply Hume's tests to the New Testament witnesses for the resurrection of Christ.

---

*That Jesus claimed to be God is evident from the following facts: (1) He allowed John to herald Him as Yahweh (a name given only to God) (Matt. 3:3); (2) He claimed His word was on a par with God's (cf. Matt. 24:35 and 5:18); (3) He claimed to be able to forgive sins, which only God can do (Mark 2:5–7); (4) He claimed to be Messiah-God of Daniel 7:13 (Mark 14:62); (5) He claimed power to raise and judge the dead (John 5:25–30); (6) He claimed he should be worshiped as God is (John 5:23); (7) He accepted worship on numerous occasions (Matt. 8:2; 9:18; John 9:38, et al.); (8) He claimed to have eternal glory with the Father (John 17:1, 5); (9) He claimed to have eternal glory with the Father (John 17:1, 5); (9) He claimed to be Yahweh of the Old Testament (cf. John 8:12 and Isa. 60:19; cf. John 10:11 and Ps. 23:1); and (10) He claimed to be the "I am" of Exodus 3:14 (John 8:58). Also see Jon A. Buell and O. Quentin Hyder, *Jesus: God, Ghost or Guru?* (Grand Rapids: Zondervan/Probe, 1978), chapter 2 and the appendix.

1. *Do the witnesses contradict each other*? The answer is: In no essential way do the witnesses contradict each other. Each New Testament writer tells part or the whole of the same story. Christ was crucified around A.D. 33 under Pontius Pilate in Jerusalem. He was confirmed to be dead and buried, and yet three days later the tomb was empty. Further, Jesus physically appeared to many groups of people on many occasions over the next month or so. He proved His reality to them so convincingly that these skeptical men boldly preached the Resurrection a little over a month later in the same city, whereupon thousands of Jews were converted to Christianity.

**Conflicts
Versus
Contradictions**

To be sure, there are minor discrepancies in the Gospel accounts. One account (Matt. 28:5) says there was one angel at the tomb; John says there were two angels there (John 20:12). But two things should be noted about these kinds of discrepancies. First, they are conflicts but not contradictions. That is, they are not irreconcilable. Matthew does not say there was *only* one angel there. That would be a contradiction. The simple rule of harmony is this: "Where there are two, there is one." Second, conflict of testimony is just what one would expect from authentic, independent witnesses. Any perceptive judge who heard several witnesses give identical word-for-word reports of a crime would throw the evidence out of court because of apparent collusion. The divergency of the Gospel accounts actually supports their authenticity. It argues for the independence of the witnesses. For if they had been in collusion, then surely they would have ironed out any apparent contradictions in their stories.

**Beyond
All
Reasonable
Doubt**

2. *Were there a sufficient number of witnesses*? The sum total of eyewitnesses to the Resurrection was over five hundred (cf. 1 Cor. 15:6). Jesus appeared to Mary (John 20:11–18), to the other women (Matt. 28:9–10), to Peter (Luke 24:34), to two disciples going to Emmaus (Luke 24:13–32), to ten apostles

(John 20:19–25), to eleven apostles (John 20:26–29), to seven apostles at the Sea of Galilee (John 21:1–14), to the eleven apostles to commission them (Matt. 28:16–20), to more than "five hundred brethren" (1 Cor. 15:6), to his unbelieving brother James (1 Cor. 15:7), and to the disciples at the ascension (Luke 24:50–53; Acts 1:4–11).

Several things about these appearances should be noted. First, there are at least eleven different appearances. Second, they were spread out over a forty-day period (Acts 1:3). Third, during these appearances Jesus performed miracles (John 20:30), engaged in teaching sessions (Acts 1:3), ate three meals (Luke 24:30, 41–43; John 21:13; Acts 10:41), proved His physical reality by showing His wounds (John 20:27), revealed His flesh and bones (Luke 24:39), and allowed His followers to touch Him (John 20:17). Finally, as a result of these appearances, a group of scared (Mark 16:8; John 20:19) and skeptical (Luke 24:38; John 20:25) men were transformed into courageous evangels who proclaimed the Resurrection in the face of threats on their lives (Acts 4:21; 5:18)!

In brief, the number of witnesses, the long time span, and the number of appearances seem to be more than sufficient to authenticate the miracle of the Resurrection beyond all *reasonable* doubt.

3. *Were the witnesses of good character?* Everything known about these witnesses—a good amount for most of them—leads to the unavoidable conclusion that they were men of the highest integrity. This is evident from the following considerations. First, their writings reflect the highest moral and ethical standards (the New Testament). Second, they were men, highly esteemed in their communities, who held leadership positions in the church.* Third, no one in the first century ever proved them to be frauds. Their message was *resisted* but their testimony was never *refuted*. Fourth, according to history, these men were

Resisted, but Not Refuted

---

*See the high qualifications for church leaders given in 1 Timothy 3:1–13.

willing to (and possibly all but one did) die for their testimony. Testimonies in the face of death are of the highest order of integrity and are so accepted in a court of law. Few if any men will die claiming something is true that they know to be false. Finally, if we cannot believe these honest disciples of Christ, then who can be believed? To reject their testimony is to cast doubt on all of history (which is based on testimony), since little (if any) history is based on testimony of quality superior to that of the New Testament.

4. *Was their testimony prejudiced*? Were the witnesses neutral, objective witnesses? Did they have "an axe to grind?" The answer to this is that the witnesses approached the original event (the appearances of the resurrected Christ) in an attitude of skepticism. They were by no means out to prove the Resurrection was true. They in fact disbelieved the early reports (Mark 16:11; Luke 24:11, 25). Another refused to believe the reports until he touched Jesus for himself (John 20:25, 27). The other dominant states of mind were fear (John 20:19) and disappointment (Luke 24:21). Fearful and doubtful they were, but prejudiced they were not.

It is sometimes objected that Jesus appeared only to believers and that no unbelievers saw Him. This is not so. Almost all were unbelieving when the report first reached them. Further, both James and Paul were not even Christians when Christ appeared to them (1 Cor. 15:7–8). Of course, all became believers *after* Christ appeared, but this does not discredit their testimony to the Resurrection. It actually supports the validity of their testimony, since the actual Resurrection is the best explanation as to why they became so firmly convinced that it was true.

5. *Were the witnesses perjurors*? This question has already been answered in the previous two points. The answer is: No, they were honest men. Their independent testimonies correspond without contradiction or collusion and stand without refutation by their contemporaries. They were never known as nor

proven to be liars. There are numerous ways to cross-check their testimony by that of others (both friend and foe) and by historical verification of other things that they claimed were true. Even if they were only men of basic (not superior) integrity, one can confidently conclude that the resurrection of Christ occurred.

Hume also suggested that all miracle accounts were given by ignorant, susceptible people in remote places. In view of the foregoing discussion, one can clearly see that, whatever weight these criticisms have for miracle stories of other religions, they certainly do not apply to the resurrection of Christ. Jesus' resurrection occurred in a major eastern city at the crossroads of the ancient world (Jerusalem) under a known Roman governor (Pilate). As the first Christian historian (Dr. Luke) recorded Paul's statement, "This has not been done in a corner" (Acts 26:26). Furthermore, there were many intelligent (even educated) witnesses to Christ's resurrection. John was from a cultured background,* Paul was highly educated (Acts 22:3), and Luke was a physician (Col. 4:14). If numerous men live with a person closely for several years, as did Jesus' disciples, they are not easily fooled.† The skepticism of the disciples rules out either susceptibility or hallucination, as do the many repeated appearances of a living person with a tangible body over a long period of time.

However, Hume's skepticism does apply appropriately to many miracle stories outside the New Testament. There are often scant, questionable, and un-

---

*John's family owned a fishing business and had servants (Mark 1:19–20; Luke 5:10). His mother gave support to Jesus and His disciples (Luke 8:2–3; John 19:25). John had political "connections" that got him into "high places" (cf. John 18:15–16). The family probably owned the large Jerusalem home that accommodated one hundred and twenty persons in one room, which is mentioned in John 19:26–27 and Acts 1:13–15.

†The apostles' testimony is of special value, because they were with Him "from the beginning" (John 15:27; cf. Acts 1:22) and hence could bear "witness" to Him in a special and intimate sense (Heb. 2:3–4; cf. Luke 1:2; Acts 10:39).

Side notes:

clear witnesses of alleged miracle events in remote areas. Further, since these stories are not of persons who claim to be God, who perform many miracles, and who predict and accomplish their own resurrection from the dead, they are not in the unique class of the great Christian miracles. In point of fact, Hume is right: all other (i.e., non-Christian) miracle claims prove nothing about the truth of their religious systems. Other contrary religious beliefs have the same kind of "miracles" to support them. But this makes their claims self-canceling. Only Christianity provides a unique set of claims and unique series of supernatural credentials to support these claims. Therefore, we believe only Christianity is miraculously confirmed to be true.

III. The Identity of the Resurrection as a Miracle

Abundant Confirmation

In chapter 9, it was concluded that miracles must be identified in terms of certain characteristics that, collectively, we called a theistic context. Miracles must be unusual events that possess theological, moral, doctrinal, and teleological dimensions. The question of who may be able to make identification is determined by the width of the circle of applicability of the theistic context. In the case of the burning bush, the circle of applicability extended only to Moses, so that he alone was able to identify the miracle. For other miracles, the theistic context was large enough to include all of Israel and Egypt. We now consider whether the circle of applicability extends to us today, so that we can make actual identification of a miracle. Let us briefly see if the resurrection of Jesus meets these tests.

Few would question the *unusual* nature of the Resurrection. Even the skeptic David Hume admitted that a resurrection would be a miracle. Virtually everyone would agree that resurrections are statistically improbable.

Likewise, no serious student of the New Testament can fail to see that the documents bear witness to the constant *theistic* context in which the life, death, and resurrection of Christ are placed (e.g., John 10:17–18). This meets the second earmark of the miracle.

There is also constant reference in the New Testament to the praise and *glory* that Christ's death and resurrection brought to God. Indeed, the voice of the Father spoke three times from heaven in approval of Christ (Matt. 3:17; 17:5; John 12:28). Jesus often referred to the glory that God would receive from His work (cf. John 17). This fits the third characteristic of a miracle.

As to the *doctrinal* dimension of the Resurrection, Jesus offered it as a proof of His claims to be the Son of God (cf. John 2:18–22; 10:18). Indeed, He offered it as *the* sign that He was of God (Matt. 12:38–40). Hence, there was not only truth content connected with the miracle of the Resurrection, but the central truth content of who He was is directly connected with His resurrection. Thus, the fourth sign of a miracle is fulfilled.

Finally, the resurrection of Christ had a *teleological* dimension. As has been pointed out, it did bring glory to God. And on the manward side, His resurrection is directly connected with our salvation. For Jesus "was delivered up because of our transgressions, and was raised because of our justification" (Rom. 4:25). In fact, Paul argues that without the Resurrection we would still be in our sins (1 Cor. 15:17).

The resurrection of Jesus satisfies all the five characteristics of a miracle. All that remains is to ask: Does the miracle of the Resurrection include, within its circle of applicability, those who are living today? To answer this, we need only note that the Resurrection is a matter of history open to any who wish to examine the evidence. Anyone who cares to examine the Gospels more carefully can find abundant confirmation of all of these points. This brief summary, however, suffices to indicate that the resurrection of Jesus can be identified as a miracle.

Miracles
and Modern
Thought

Summary:
Miracles
Are
Actual

To summarize the results of our study, we may conclude that (1) miracles are identifiable in a theistic universe, (2) the Bible provides us with the identifying characteristics of a miracle, and (3) the resurrection of Christ possesses these characteristics. Therefore, a miracle can be identified as having occurred. Miracles are not only possible, but they are actual.

The question of the actuality of miracles is a historical one. Ancient history is based on documents and witnesses. As a historical document, the New Testament is of superior quality. There are more manuscript copies of better quality and of an earlier date of the New Testament than of any other book from antiquity. History is also dependent on firsthand information. Here too the miracles and resurrection of Christ have more honest and capable witnesses than any other events of the ancient world. What is witnessed is an event that fits all the characteristics of a miracle. Hence, a miracle has been identified as actual.

For those who have a Christian theistic world view, these arguments have encouraging implications. They indicate that the theistic view is sound and viable, indeed, that it is the truth of what is! The logical reasoning and historical inquiry demonstrated here not only corroborate the biblical evidence but they also indicate the correspondence of the whole theistic system to reality. The ultimate tests of a world view are these: Does it correspond to reality? Does it meet *all* the needs of the *person*?

For those with a naturalistic world view, on the other hand, these arguments represent a challenge. If there are no telling arguments against miracles, if naturalism is not necessarily true, then it is possible that supernaturalism *is* true. The question then, is this: Does a naturalistic world view meet all your needs, or is it lacking? Does it meet your personal, spiritual, and eternal needs? Consider the alternatives.

Miracles can happen, and at least one *did* happen.

Response

The issue of the role of miracle touches the eye of the tornado that rages between classical Christianity and secular systems of philosophy. It focuses the debate on those points that sharply divide the naturalist and the supernaturalist. The issue is not simple but complex, spanning several academic disciplines, including those of philosophy, theology, history, natural science, and ethics.

R. C. SPROUL

In this astute treatment of the key debates, modern and historic, that center on miracles, Dr. Geisler cuts through the snarled threads of argumentation to lay bare the core intellectual issues involved. All of the chief objections to miracle are carefully examined and countered. The myth that "miracle" belongs to the sphere of faith, banished from the arena of rational inquiry, is exploded. Unhappily, however, the myth will surely continue to live and grow, as do the heads of a hydra, as objections to Christianity continue and are nurtured by the reluctance of Christians to counter them with sound intellectual evidence.

Since the Kantian watershed consigned miracle to the realm of the unknowable or incredible, many Christians have abandoned the debate, unnecessarily surrendering the weapons of reason and empirical investigation to the arsenals of the skeptic. Hiding behind a mystical type of evidenceless "faith," these Christians have believed that rational inquiry into miracles would be futile at best and impious at worst. They have substituted credulity for credibility, giving some justification for the skeptics' contempt for their faith.

Norman Geisler refuses to capitulate to the Kantian form of metaphysical agnosticism, which serves as the substructure for so much of modern naturalism. He duels with the skeptics on their own turf, turning their epistemologies on themselves, arguing in the effective classical mode of *ad hominem* reasoning

155

(without committing the informal fallacy of *ad hominem abusive*).

His work shows where the advocates of rationalism abandon sound reason in their attack on miracle, violating their own commitment to logic and inferential deduction by repeatedly committing the *petitio principii* fallacy. He demonstrates how the empiricists must repudiate their own assumptions (which are necessary for the scientific method) in order to combat miracle. Again and again, from Spinoza to Flew, Geisler reveals the arbitrary character of the arguments used to repudiate biblical Christianity.

An important aspect of Geisler's work is his clarification of the complexities involved in the miracle question. That the issue cannot be resolved simplistically by blind appeals to faith or science is made manifest. Rather, it is clear that the question touches heavily on prior issues of metaphysics, causality, historiography, and ethics.

It is refreshing in our times to see a Christian scholar emerge who is not afraid to debate the issues and the truth claims of Christianity *in the marketplace*. Geisler is a marketplace apologist who refuses to practice his faith only in closed chambers of some spiritual "upper room."

References

[1]Ludwig Feuerbach, quoted by Karl Barth in "An Introductory Essay" to Feuerbach, *The Essence of Christianity* (New York: Harper, 1957), p. xi.

[2]Thomas Huxley, *The Works of T. H. Huxley* (New York: Appleton, 1896), p. 153.

[3]As quoted in the *International Standard Bible Encyclopedia* (Grand Rapids: Eerdmans, 1939), p. 2063.

[4]Benedict De Spinoza, *Tractatus Theologico-Politicus*, in *The Chief Works of Benedict de Spinoza*, trans. R. H. M. Elwes (London: George Bell and Sons, 1883), 1:83, 87, 92.

[5]Ibid., p. 83.

[6]Ibid., p. 92.

[7]Ibid., p. 83.

[8]Ibid., p. 87.

[9]Benedict De Spinoza, *Ethics*, ed. James Gutmann (New York: Hafner, 1949), pt. 1, pp. 41–42.

[10]Spinoza, *Tractatus*, p. 126.

[11]Ibid., pp. 129–30.

[12]Ibid., p. 170.

[13]Ibid., p. 165.

[14]Ibid., pp. 172, 196–97.

[15]Spinoza, *Ethics*, pt. 1, proposition XXXVI, appendix.

[16]Spinoza, *Tractatus*, p. 92.

[17]Ibid., p. 96.

[18]Ibid., p. 159. Spinoza sometimes says the prophets spoke by "revelation" but understands this as the "extraordinary power . . . [of] the imagination of the prophet" (ibid., p. 24).

[19]Robert Jastrow, *God and the Astronomers* (New York: Norton, 1978), p. 15.

[20]Ibid., p. 16.

[21]Ibid., p. 25.

[22]Ibid., p. 27.

[23]Ibid., p. 28.

[24]Ibid.

[25]William James, *Some Problems of Philosophy* (New York: Longmans, Green, 1911), p. 40.

[26]C. F. von Weizsäcker, *The Relevance of Science* (New York: Harper & Row, 1964), p. 36.

[27]Jastrow, *God and the Astronomers*, pp. 111–12.

[28]Ibid., p. 112.

[29]Ibid., p. 113.

[30]Ibid.

[31]Ibid., p. 116.

[32]David Hume, *An Inquiry Concerning Human Understanding*, ed. C. W. Hendel (New York: Bobbs-Merrill, 1955), sec. 4. pt. 1, p. 40 (hereafter called *Inquiry*).

[33]Ibid., 12. 3. 173.

[34]Ibid., 4. 1. 41.

[35]Ibid., 5. 1. 57.

[36]Ibid.

[37]Ibid., 6. 1. 69.

[38]Ibid., 7. 2. 85.

[39]Ibid., 10. 1. 118.

[40]Ibid.

[41]Ibid.

[42]Ibid., 10. 1. 120.

[43]Ibid.

[44]Ibid.

[45]Ibid.

[46]Ibid., 10. 1. 121.

[47]Ibid., 10. 1. 122.

[48]Ibid.

[49]Ibid., 10. 1. 123.

[50]Ibid., 10. 1. 122–23.

[51]C. S. Lewis, *Miracles* (New York: Macmillan, 1969), p. 105.

[52]*Inquiry*, 10. 1. 118.

[53]Ibid., 10. 1. 123.

[54]Ibid., 10. 1. 122.

[55] Richard Whately, *Historical Doubts Concerning the Existence of Napoleon Bonaparte*, in *Famous Pamphlets*, 2d ed., ed. Henry Morley (London: George Routledge and Sons, 1890), pp. 274, 290. Also published as *Historical Doubts Relative to Napoleon Bonaparte* (New York: Robert Caster and Bros., 1849).

[56] *Inquiry*, 10. 1. 118.

[57] David Hume, *An Abstract of a Treatise on Human Nature*, 1740 ed. (Cambridge: Cambridge University Press, 1938), pp. 14–16.

[58] *The Encyclopedia of Philosophy*, s.v. "Miracles," by Antony Flew.

[59] Ibid.

[60] Antony Flew, "Theology and Falsification," in *The Existence of God*, ed. John Hick (New York: Macmillan, 1964), p. 227.

[61] George D. Chryssides, "Miracles and Agents," *Religious Studies* 11 (September 1975): 319–27.

[62] Ibid., p. 321.

[63] Ibid., p. 319.

[64] Ibid., p. 322.

[65] Ibid., p. 325.

[66] Ibid., p. 326

[67] Ibid., p. 327.

[68] Ibid., p. 325.

[69] *Inquiry*, 10. 1. 122.

[70] Patrick Nowell-Smith, "Miracles," in *New Essays in Philosophical Theology*, ed. Antony Flew and Alasdair MacIntyre (New York: Macmillan, 1955), pp. 245–46.

[71] Ibid., p. 246.

[72] Ibid., p. 247.

[73] Ibid., p. 248.

[74] Ibid., p. 249.

[75] Ibid., p. 251.

[76] Ibid., p. 253.

[77] Ibid.

[78] Ibid., p. 243.

[79] Ibid., p. 247.

[80] Ibid., p. 248.

[81] Ibid., p. 251.

[82] Malcolm L. Diamond, "Miracles," *Religious Studies* 9 (September 1973): 316–17.

[83] Ninian Smart, *Philosophers and Religious Truth* (London: SCM, 1964), p. 41.

[84] Guy Robinson, quoted in Diamond, "Miracles," p. 317.

[85] Diamond, "Miracles," p. 320.

[86] Ibid., p. 321.

[87] Ibid.

[88] See Fred Hoyle and N. C. Wickramasinghe, *Evolution From Space* (London: Dent, 1981), pp. 24, 94, 147.

[89] See Norman Geisler, *Christian Apologetics* (Grand Rapids: Baker, 1976), chap. 12, for further discussion of this point.

[90] Diamond, "Miracles," p. 321.

[91] A. N. Whitehead, *Science and the Modern World* (1925; reprint ed., New York: Free Press, 1967), chaps. 1, 11.

[92] Ian Barbour, *Issues in Science and Religion* (Englewood Cliffs, N.J.: Prentice Hall, 1966).

[93] Flew, "Miracles," p. 346.

[94] Thomas Aquinas *Summa contra Gentiles* 3. 100.

[95] Eric Mascall quoted in Flew, "Miracles," p. 346.

[96] Flew, "Miracles," p. 347.

[97] Ibid.

[98] Quoted in Flew, "Miracles," p. 347.

[99] Augustine *City of God* 21. 8.

[100] Flew, "Miracles," p. 348.

[101] Ibid.

[102] Ibid., pp. 348–49.

[103] John W. Montgomery, *History and Christianity* (Downers Grove, Ill.: InterVarsity, 1964), p. 75.

[104] Montgomery, *The Shape of the Past* (Minneapolis: Bethany, 1962), p. 140.

[105] Montgomery, *History and Christianity*, p. 88.

[106] Cornelius Van Til, *Defense of the Faith* (Philadelphia: Presbyterian and Reformed, 1955), p. 118.

[107] Hume, *The Letters of David Hume*, ed. J. Y. T. Grieg (Oxford, 1932), 1:187.

[108] Jastrow, *Astronomers*, pp. 106–8.

[109] See William Craig, *The Existence of God and the Beginning of the Universe* (San Bernardino: Here's Life, 1979) for further discussion of this point.

[110] Bertrand Russell, "A Debate on the Existence of God," in *The Existence of God*, ed. John Hick (New York: Macmillan, 1964), pp. 174–75.

[111] Paul Kurtz, ed., *The Humanist Manifestos I and II* (Buffalo, N.Y.: Prometheus, 1973), pp. 18–19.

[112] Rudolf Bultmann, *Kerygma and Myth: A Theological Debate*, ed. Hans Werner Bartsch, trans. Reginald H. Fuller (London: Billing and Sons, 1954), p. 1.

[113] Ibid., p. 2.

[114] Ibid., p. 3.

[115] Ibid., pp. 3–4.

[116] Ibid., p. 4.

[117] Ibid., p. 5.

[118] Ibid., p. 7.

[119] Ibid., p. 8.

[120] Ibid., pp. 10–11.

[121] Ibid., p. 12.

[122] Ibid., p. 34.

[123] Ibid., pp. 38–39.

[124] Ibid., pp. 39–40.

[125] Ibid., p. 40.

[126] Ibid., p. 42

[127] Ibid.

[128] Ibid., p. 39.

[129] Ibid.

[130] Flew, "Theology and Falsification," p. 227.

[131] *Encyclopedia of Religion and Ethics*, s.v. "Historiography," by E. Troeltsch.

[132] Carl Becker, "Detachment and the Writing of History," in *Detachment and the Writing of History*, ed. Phil L. Snyder (Westport, Conn.: Greenwood Press. 1972), pp. 12–13.

[133] F. H. Bradley, *The Presuppositions of Critical History* (Chicago: Quadrangle, 1968), p. 100.

[134] See Hume's *Treatise*, 2. 3. 1. and *Inquiry*, 8.

[135] Flew, "Miracles," p. 350.

[136] Ibid., p. 351.

[137] Ibid., p. 352.

[138] Ibid.

[139] Jastrow, *Astronomers*, p. 113.

[140] Ibid., p. 112.

[141] Ibid.

[142] Ibid., p. 28.

[143] Ibid., p. 27.

[144] Erlandson, "A New Look," *Religious Studies*, vol. 3, no. 4 (December 1977), pp. 417–28.

[145] Whately, "Doubts Concerning Napoleon," pp. 224, 290.

[146] See Friedrich Schleiermacher, *On Religion: Speeches to Its Cultured Despisers*, trans. John Oman (New York: Harper Torchbooks, 1958); and Adolf Harnack, *What is Christianity?* trans. Thomas B. Saunders (New York: Harper Torchbooks, 1957).

[147] Robert M. Hutchins, ed., *Great Books of the Western World* (Chicago: Encyclopaedia Britannica, 1952), vol. 23 (*Machiavelli/Hobbes*): *Leviathan,* by Thomas Hobbes, p. 80.

[148] Ibid.

[149] Ibid., pp. 82–83.

[150] Ibid., p. 83.

[151] Ibid., p. 70.

[152] Ibid., pp. 70–71.

[153] Ibid., p. 165.

[154] See Immanuel Kant, *Critique of Pure Reason*, 2d ed., trans. Norman K. Sinith (New York: St. Martin, 1965).

[155] See Kant, *Critique of Practical Reason* (New York: Bobbs-Merrill, 1956).

[156] See Kant, *Religion Within the Limits of Reason Alone*, 2d ed., trans. T. M. Greene and H. H. Hudson (New York: Harper Torchbooks, 1960).

[157] Ibid., pp. 100–101.

[158] Ibid., p. 104.

[159] Ibid., pp. 98, 103.

[160] Ibid.

[161] Ibid., pp. 79–80.

[162]Ibid., p. 179.

[163]Ibid., p. 82.

[164]Ibid., pp. 83–84.

[165]Ibid., p. 83.

[166]Ibid., p. 119.

[167]See Kant, *Pure Reason*.

[168]See Kant, *Practical Reason*.

[169]Kant, *Religion Within the Limits of Reason Alone*, p. 82.

[170]John 20:30–31.

[171]For further discussion of moral conflicts, see Geisler, *Ethics: Alternatives and Issues* (Grand Rapids: Zondervan, 1971), especially chaps. 5–7.

[172]Compare Exodus 9:29–30; 10:1–2.

[173]Compare Exodus 5:1; 6:7; 11:7.

[174]See also Deuteronomy 29:2–3; Joshua 24:17; Nehemiah 9:10; Psalm 105:27; Jeremiah 32:20–21.

[175]Also in Deuteronomy 4:34; 7:19; 13:1, 2; 28:46; 29:3; 34:11; Nehemiah 9:10; Psalm 135:9; Jeremiah 32:20–21.

[176]Also in Exodus 11:9–10; Psalm 78:43; 105:27; Joel 2:30.

[177]Also in Deuteronomy 8:17; Nahum 2:1.

[178]See also Jeremiah 27:5; 32:17; 51:15.

[179]Also used in Exodus 32:11; Deuteronomy 4:37; 2 Kings 17:36; Nehemiah 1:10.

[180]Compare Deuteronomy 7:19; 26:8; 34:12.

[181]Used once of a satanic sign in 2 Thessalonians 2:9.

[182]Also so used in Mark 13:22; Acts 2:19.

[183]See also Acts 4:30; 5:12; Hebrews 2:3–4.

[184]Compare Acts 15:12; Romans 15:19.

[185]Colin Brown, ed., *Dictionary of New Testament Theology*, (Grand Rapids: Zondervan, 1976), 2:633.

[186]Ibid., pp. 623–25. See parallel word for "wonder" (*thauma*).

[187]For further experiential indications of demonic influence in the world today, see Kurt Koch, *Between Christ and Satan* (Grand Rapids: Kregel, 1961).

[188]See also Matthew 5:17; Luke 24:27, 44; John 5:39; Hebrews 10:7.

[189]*The Protevangelium of James* 18.2. Unless otherwise stated, all references to apocryphal books are from *New*

Testament Apocrypha, ed. Edgar Hennecke, 2 vols. (Philadelphia: Westminster, 1963).

[190]*The Infancy Story of Thomas* 2. 1–4; 3. 1–3.

[191]Ibid., 5. 1.

[192]Ibid., 13. 1–2.

[193]As quoted by B. B. Warfield in *Counterfeit Miracles* (New York: Scribner, 1918), pp. 66–67.

[194]Ibid., p. 251.

[195]Ibid., p. 269.

[196]Ibid., p. 262.

[197]Ibid., p. 274.

[198]Jacques Douillet, *What Is a Saint?* (New York: Hawthorn, 1958), pp. 63, 100.

[199]Lewis, *Miracles*, p. 132.

[200]Ibid.

[201]Ibid., p. 140.

[202]Ibid., p. 141.

[203]Ibid., p. 142.

[204]Ibid.

[205]Ibid.

[206]Ibid., p. 143.

[207]Ibid., p. 157.

[208]Ibid., pp. 112ff. (This is Lewis's apt description.)

[209]Ibid., p. 132.

[210]Hume, *Inquiry*, p. 124.

[211]Ibid., pp. 125–26.

[212]Ibid., pp. 126–28.

[213]Ibid., pp. 129–30.

[214]Ibid., p. 137.

[215]Ibid., p. 133.

[216]Ibid., p. 129.

[217]F. F. Bruce, *The New Testament Documents: Are They Reliable?* (Grand Rapids: Eerdmans, 1965), p. 16.

[218]John Rylands papyri (P52), dated A.D. 114.

[219]Norman L. Geisler and William E. Nix, *A General Introduction to the Bible* (Chicago: Moody, 1968), p. 365.

[220]Ibid., pp. 365–66.

[221] Bruce Metzger, *Chapters in the History of New Testament Textual Criticism* (Grand Rapids: Eerdmans, 1963).

[222] Frederic Kenyon, *Our Bible and the Ancient Manuscripts*, 4th ed. (New York: Harper, 1958), p. 55.

[223] *McCormick's Handbook of the Law of Evidence*, 2d ed. (St. Paul, Minn.: West, 1972), sec. 223.

[224] See John W. Montgomery, *The Law Above the Law* (Minneapolis: Bethany, 1975).

[225] Nelson Glueck, *Rivers in the Desert: a History of the Negev* (Philadephia: Jewish Publication Society, 1969), p. 136.

[226] Interview with William F. Albright, *Christianity Today*, 18 January 1963, p. 359.

[227] See John A. T. Robinson, *Honest to God* (Philadelphia: Westminster, 1963).

[228] See John A. T. Robinson, *Redating the New Testament* (Philadelphia: Westminster, 1976).

[229] William Ramsay, *St. Paul the Traveller and the Roman Citizen* (New York: Putnam, 1896), p. 8.

[230] Hume, *Inquiry*, p. 120.

For Further Reading

Augustine **City of God** 21. 6–8; 22. 8–10.

The classic statement of miracles as irregular exceptions to the regular patterns of nature is made by Augustine in this book. It is the basis for much of the traditional Christian apologetic for miracles.

Bube, Richard, ed. **Journal of American Scientific Affiliation**, December 1978, several articles.

A good interchange by J. W. Montgomery and the Basinger brothers on the apologetic value of miracles is included in these articles written by contemporary evangelical scholars.

Campbell, George. **A Dissertation on Miracles**. 1762. Reprint. London: T. Tegg & Son, 1834.

This is a reply to David Hume by a famous Scottish theologian of his day.

Clarke, Samuel. **The Works of Samuel Clarke**. Vol. 2. London, 1738.

This book is an answer to the objection to miracles arising out of the philosophies of Hobbes and Spinoza.

Lewis, C. S. **God in the Dock**. Grand Rapids: Eerdmans, 1970. Chapters 2, 8, and 9.

This book contains several excellent and insightful chapters on miracles.

_____. **Miracles**. New York: Macmillan, 1947.

This is the best overall apologetic for miracles written in this century.

Morison, Frank. **Who Moved the Stone?** Grand Rapids: Zondervan, 1976.

A converted skeptic who had sought to disprove the miracle of the Resurrection has written this unique defense of the event.

Paley, William. **A View of the Evidences of Christianity**. "Prefactory Considerations," 1794.

A classic eighteenth-century response to the deistic denial of miracles.

Smart, Ninian. **Philosophers and Religious Truth**. London: SCM, 1964. Chapter 2.

This contribution is a significant answer to the criticism that miracles are unscientific.

Swinburne, Richard. **The Concept of Miracle**. London: Macmillan, 1970.

One of the best philosophical defenses of miracles written in this generation.

Tennant, F. R. **Miracle and Its Philosophical Presuppositions**. Cambridge: Cambridge University Press, 1925.

This is an important work by the late Cambridge philosopher of religion. It gives a rational defense of miracles and of the supernatural in the Anglican tradition. It is less conservative than C. S. Lewis.

Thomas Aquinas. **Summa contra Gentiles** 3. 98–103.

Aquinas defends the strong concept of miracle as a violation of natural law. This is perhaps the best representation of classic theism.

Warfield, B. B. **Counterfeit Miracles**. New York: Scribner, 1918.

This book argues strongly for apostolic miracles and against miracles after the period.

Whately, Richard. **Historical Doubts Relative to Napoleon Bonaparte**. New York: Robert Caster, 1849.

Whately satirizes David Hume's famous attack on miracles, claiming that Hume's views would eliminate historical knowledge of other unique (nonmiraculous) events of the past.